# CRADLED IN CHRISTADELPHIA

# CRADLED IN CHRISTADELPHIA

Reflections on a Happy Childhood in the
Christadelphian Community during the
1920/30s

Ruth McHaffie
(1920-2004)

2014

Written in gratitude to my parents, the extended family,
my school teachers, Sunday School teachers
and all the "meeting" people
who ensured that I had a happy, contented childhood.

Illustrations, except where indicated otherwise, have been
contributed by my art student grandson, Ben McHaffie.

2004

CRADLED IN CHRISTADELPHIA

ISBN 978-0-9546681-3-6

Published by Ian & Averil McHaffie, 176 Granton Road,
Edinburgh EH5 1AH
mchaffie@tesco.net
2014

# CRADLED IN CHRISTADELPHIA

## TABLE OF CONTENTS

# Appendices

# PREFACE

Ruth McHaffie, my mother, completed the text for this volume a few days before she died on 6th March 2004. She had arranged for her grandson, Ben, to produce some drawings and had seen and approved these, and had chosen a few photographs and the cover designs. Had she lived longer, we would have worked together to select further photographs, but that not proving possible, I have selected from photographs available, placing them where they would help to illustrate the text.

Mum also intended to include appendices, but she did not leave clear instructions as to what she had in mind. I have therefore chosen a few items which illustrate aspects of her life and writing, and have also added some family-tree charts so that relationships can more easily be understood.

The wording in some of Mum's sentences could probably be improved, and had she had time, this would have been done. She would probably also have updated and corrected the confusing usage of the archaic term "Brethren". Sometimes it is used to mean "Brothers and Sisters" (i.e. members of the Christadelphian community). At other times it means "Brothers" not "Sisters". However, we all used to use this term in this misleading way in the past, and some still do, so I have not sought to update it in this book.

While mum was failing in health she worked particularly hard to finish her two-volumed work *Timewatching and Israel*. In this she explained and supported an understanding of the Bible and of world events in a way she felt very important. It was still at the printers when she died, and has subsequently been distributed. Her autobiographical writings regrettably have had to wait. They were produced partly for historical interest and entertainment, but since they were also intended to serve a spiritual purpose, it seems appropriate to finish each volume with one of the prayers she wrote for publication.

I had hoped to be able to arrange these works for printing much sooner, but life has been very busy. I can only apologise to those who ordered copies that there has been such a lengthy delay. I am pleased to have been asked (gently) many times when these books would be available, and hope that those who have waited so long will not be disappointed on receiving the finished product.

It was always a pleasure for me to work with mum, to proofread her articles, to discuss and debate the content, and to help with the computing side of the publication. I feel privileged to have been brought up by parents who took a great interest in all their children's activities, and who encouraged and challenged us in every way, including spiritually. We could discuss anything with them and we did so. They have left us a valuable legacy, and it is a delight to be able to continue their spiritual influence by seeing these writings through to publication.

Ian McHaffie

# I
# INTRODUCTION

The gentle and unassuming author, Islip Collyer, once wrote:

... although we are all ready to criticise the man of modest attainments who ventures on anything in the nature of an autobiography, it is nevertheless a fact that nothing interests us more.

With that comment in mind and though keenly aware of my "modest attainments", I am venturing to tell something of my life during early years. Many contemporaries could relate more exciting and more worthy adventures, and whether or not this story will succeed in being of interest or prove dreadfully dull must, of course, be left for readers to decide. Although my presentation will be more intelligible to members of the Christadelphian community into which I was born and nurtured, possibly it will 'ring a bell' for others who have been reared in one or other of the small non-conformist groups.

The indulgence of readers must be requested for the sometimes trivial comments which have been included. Members of two generations in our family have pressed me to write, and the little everyday things are added mainly for the grandchildren and their children whose life-styles are so different from my own. Which trivialities were to be included has been determined by whether or not I would have liked to learn of them if I were reading of my own great-grandparents. Several times while looking through the pages before publication I have thought to myself "So what?" and "How boring can I get!". But the passing of the years has a strange way of adding interest or amusement to the "changing scenes of life" however dull they seem at the time – as evidenced by some of the material presented in TV "memory lane" programmes.

In a companion book entitled *Reformation and Renewal* I have concentrated largely on the life and conclusions of my husband George (1920-1985) who was also reared in the Christadelphian community – he in Edinburgh, and I in London. That, too, has been written in response to requests, and inevitably covers our joint experiences. In it I have endeavoured to give an explanation to those who have been puzzled as to how it was that we developed in the way we did. Because during the whole of our lifetimes we have both been so involved in affairs relating to Christianity especially within the Christadelphian body, it is inevitable that our activities and the problems we encountered quite often dominate my subject matter, especially in the second book.

A number of Christadelphians harbour the idea that in their talks and writings there is something wrong if lessons are drawn from personal experiences, and that they themselves should remain "faceless". Illustrations must only be taken from the Scriptures. This seems a pity, for we can gain usefully from the experiences of each other, whether we learn from the spoken or written words. To know that someone else felt as we did in comparable circumstances, that someone else had similar imperfections and disadvantages, that someone else was equally or more silly and had difficulty in coping, has often given others courage to face life's perplexities. Possibly the accounts which I have composed might "fill a little space" in one or another of those areas.

Some Christadelphians will, almost inevitably, ponder of the author, "Who does she think she is?" The answer is simple. She thinks, indeed knows, that she is one of a number who have been reared among them, and whose lives have followed similar patterns to her own. But, unlike her, not all have had the "bonus" of living well-past their allotted threescore years and ten, and seen years of retirement offering time to write, as well as having the advantages of the technology which, with its desk-top publishing, has enabled amateurs to produce work which at least *looks* presentable. We have travelled a long way since the first carbon paper was introduced in London in 1806 "for producing duplicates of writings". Perhaps the aphorism sometimes quoted from Patrick Kavanagh is appropriate to my effort – "the self serves only as an example". I have tried to add colour by placing my memoirs in their historical context, and am grateful for the help of authors both inside and outside our community who have supplied background information which illustrates the milieu in which I and my contemporaries were reared.

It was, I think, the theologian, John Hick, who commented that it is with red faces that many of us recall occasions in our youth. So maybe I am not alone when looking back over life as though it were a video cassette, I realise with regret that so often I could have done better, and wish the cry could be answered "Cut! I want to do that scene again". But perhaps one of the purposes of life lies in it being a learning experience, and at least we have imbibed a lesson of value and grown in wisdom if we can be critical of ourselves – and sometimes laugh at our absurdities which once seemed so sensible. As one philosopher has concluded – "We live life forwards, but understand it backwards".

The grandson of Charles Darwin once remarked that he would like to have known more of how his grandfather thought and worked. While in our family there has been nothing of the fame nor infamy attributed to Charles Darwin, yet often I wish I had asked my grandparents more about their early lives, their parents and relatives, and I'm sorry that they volunteered so little. Now that I am old, or more euphemistically a "senior citizen", I enjoy hearing of life's pattern before I was born, and would especially like to know more of the pursuits of my forebears, however commonplace, instead of having only scanty knowledge of their occupations – the publishing, the engraving and French polishing in London, the lace and shoe-making, the market gardening, Methodist lay-preaching, and the fun of bonfires at Marlow on the thick ice of the frozen Thames during Victorian winters. I have been able to add to my recollections some material which I have learned from our children who gathered it for themselves from their two grannies and from their one grandad who lived long enough to enjoy them.

Owing to a "find" in the National Library of Scotland by our eldest son, we were quite impressed to discover that he and his siblings could boast of a great-great-great-grandfather born some years before the French Revolution – an honour, it must be admitted shared with quite a number! However, in 1846 our distant Grandpa Sparkhall wrote and published a substantial booklet, in which he protested against the "free trade" advocated by the Anti-Corn-Law League, and expressed his fear that it would be detrimental not only to Britain's industries but also to the "large portion" of the population who were, as he wrote, "emaciated, squalid, careworn and poverty-stricken". As there was a considerable flutter of protests written at that time on the same subject, his effort scarcely adds notoriety. But as we can find no other publication by any predecessor, we have to make do with that as our ancestral literary heritage.[1]

In view of frequent references in the following pages to the little-known Christadelphian church, perhaps some introductory explanation is necessary for any "outside" readers. In many ways the small community with its large name (meaning "Brethren in Christ") is similar to many other dissenting groups, and sprang from the same rootstock. It often refers to its beliefs as "the Truth", with or without a capital "T", and into that "Truth" adult immersion (after a careful doctrinal examination) is considered essential. There is a depth of dedication among the members and while some converts are made from outside, its continuance in the western world is mostly dependent on one generation passing on its beliefs to the next, with inter-marrying, as well as loyalty to family and the friendships formed in childhood. In common with others claiming allegiance to Christ, its size is sinking in the West, but as we see 'the leaves around us falling' in Britain, numbers are rising in the southern hemisphere, largely due to the missionary work which has been accomplished in the last fifty or so years.

Although Christadelphian history has seen bitter disruptions when members have been divided between supporting one influential leader or another, and when the

---

[1] Title page: "*A Broad Hint to the Manufacturers, on the Subject of Corn, Coals, Steam, and Machinery, or a First Impression from a Seal Intended for the Lips of the Free-Trade Advocates* by Edward Sparkhall, London, published by the author, 142 Cheapside" (1846). See family tree on page 54.

liking or disliking of personalities has carried more weight than the average member's understanding of the particular problem under discussion, there has also been, and still is, a strong element of caring for those "within". In more recent years a need has been felt for the community to help "outsiders", though not without opposition. As with other groups, first generation Christadelphians (in the second half of the 19th century) maintained a stronger, all-over enthusiasm and kept stricter separation from the world than in the late twentieth and early twenty-first centuries, and there is now a higher proportion of members who continue to belong to their birth community more out habit or for social and family reasons than out of a desire to play an active, proselyting role.

World-wide, the extent of the continuing loyalty of oncoming generations to whichever church or group cradled them is, of course, an unknown factor. By now, dedication to any organized Christianity has been largely phased out in European culture, especially in Britain. Present-day secular education invites children to think for themselves and to discard beliefs presented "on a plate". At the same time there is pressure from peers to conform, with the media strongly influencing life-styles. Deterioration of morals in our society is often deplored but in many ways Britain at the beginning of the 21st century is a better place than the one in which I was reared, and much more so than the one which my parents and grandparents knew before me. Many have more opportunity and wider experiences, so that the unsophisticated pleasures enjoyed by myself and my contemporaries would seem to our descendants like boredom ad infinitum. But it is just possible, if the years roll on as they have done since the world began, that some young person of the future, ever mastering the latest wonders of technological science, might find this old story in an attic, brush off the dust, and settle down in a corner to read of how "they" used to think and conduct themselves "then". Possibly through these pages he or she will be helped to realise that materialism, consumerism and all that they carry with them are of ephemeral value, that they are not essential to happiness and their attractiveness wears thin as life goes on. Nobody lives through their years without meeting problems, some greater than others, some devastating. The ghastly suffering which many have endured in man-created terrors and in the natural disasters to which each succeeding century has borne witness have revealed that those with faith in a caring Being could rise above squalor and agony, could lift their eyes from the mud and see the stars, despite horrendous circumstances. And death itself has been faced with greater equanimity than by those whose lives were "self-supported".

I look back on many joyful family gatherings over the years when smiles were on every face, and I remember dancing round with bright-eyed grandchildren, singing as we went, "Everybody's happy now". That's a pretty song and altogether suitable for the nursery, but never universally true for we exist in a sorrowing and often tragic world, with many a dear one lost, and the happiness of those close to them sadly diminished. What could I wish more than that joy would for ever remain for all our grandchildren, now grown so large, and for their own infants who are already opening wide eyes on our puzzling planet? But inevitably shadows will fall and realistically I could not hold a greater wish for them and for the generations which in the normal course of events will follow, than that they should find a deep understanding of spiritual values which, though all else be lost, will yet remain.

Much of this narrative is written in appreciation of the devotion of my parents and our extended family, my day-school teachers together with the church ("the meeting" people as I learned to call the Christadelphians), who, even if they lacked prosperity, willingly gave all they could of themselves and of their time to ensure that I had a stable and contented childhood. And even more importantly, in their several ways, they set my feet on the firm foundation of a faith in God. They ensured that I had an anchor which would stay secure though fierce should be the storm, an anchor holding fast until life shall ebb away and hopefully death shall be "swallowed up" in victory.

# II
# "THE END
# IS WHERE WE START FROM"

My story is of a child with average ability, brought up in an ordinary, working-class home, but nevertheless within the fold of an extra-ordinary community. Perhaps it can be said that like most children (and like that community together with many others), when I was 'good I was very very good, but when I was bad I was horrid'.

In the spring of 1920, less than two years after the end of the First World War, I was born in the London suburb of Crouch End. Naturally I was unaware of the gigantean tragedy which so recently had caused the deaths of over ten million Europeans and 115,000 Americans, with twice as many wounded,[2] and which left in its trail immeasurable grief for widows and relatives without subsistence. Following an announcement of the Armistice on 11th November 1918, the prime minister, Lloyd George, had described the catastrophe as "the cruellest and most terrible war that has ever scourged mankind". But more tragedy had been added as the "Spanish flu" epidemic swept across the world, including the troops, and caused more than twice the total number of deaths inflicted by the hostilities. Nevertheless, the survivors in Britain celebrated her victory. They crowded the streets throughout the length and breadth of the land, danced, and shouted. Flags were waved, and "Land of Hope and Glory" was bellowed in triumph. In London, King George V came out on to the balcony of Buckingham Palace in response to the chanting of the crowds. The fountains in Trafalgar Square cascaded again and the street lights shone forth once more. Big Ben, whose chimes had been heard from the clock tower

---

[2] Garraty and Gay, *The University History of the World*, p. 992

7

of the Houses of Parliament since 1859 but silenced during the gloomy years, renewed its boom and added to the mood of celebration. And the men soon to return from the indescribable horrors which they had endured were promised a country fit "for heroes to live in".

When I was seven months old and surveying my little world from the safety of my mother's arms, there was carried to Westminster Abbey in awesome ceremony, and in the presence of a vast throng of bereaved parents and grieving widows, the body of an unknown soldier, borne from the wasted battlefields back to his homeland, the representative of Britain's unidentifiable dead. The onlookers, clad as best they could afford by the well-established "mourning warehouses", watched the scene with aching hearts. Though the Armistice had been declared, and the nation had rejoiced, yet each sorrowing soul was left with devastating emptiness. As one mourner said when she was told, so jubilantly, that the war was over, "Yes, but Hughie will not be coming back". As the cortege passed them on that memorable November morning, anguished parents would have wondered whether beneath the grandeur lay all that remained of the child for whom such high hopes had been held, and many a grieving widow would have wondered whether, hidden there, lay the shattered remains of the strong arm on which she yearned once more to lean.

On the same day in the same year (1920), as Big Ben struck the last stroke of the eleventh hour, and in the presence of yet another throng, a monumental empty tomb, the Cenotaph, was officially unveiled in Whitehall by the revered King. By July of the previous year a temporary memorial had been constructed made from wood and plaster, in readiness for the victory parade. And later, at the first anniversary of the peace declaration, crowds had spontaneously surged around it and observed two minutes silence in memory of those who had died in "the war to end war". But by November 1920 the Cenotaph had been reconstructed in white Portland stone and thereafter became the focal point of a national Day of Remembrance. Long would it be recalled of those terrifying years, as the contemporary poet wrote,

8

In Flanders' fields the poppies blow,
Between the crosses, row on row.

**The Cenotaph, Whitehall, London**

My parents, though they had survived the catastrophe,
benefited nothing from Britain's brief postwar boom which

9

added wealth only to the privileged few. But neither did they suffer the worst effects of the slump which followed in 1921 and which brought unemployment and dire poverty for many, their deprivation alleviated only by the scantiest of relief from public funds. Like those around them, my father and mother would have heard of the League of Nations which was formalised three months before my birth, and which was intended to develop international co-operation. But also like their neighbours, they would have paid little attention (even had they heard of it) to the monstrous plan drawn up by a small group of dissidents in Munich a few weeks later, a plan which would lead to the bloodshed of nearly fifty million and the misery of millions more.

Just as I had no knowledge of those depressing matters I was equally unaware of the variety of churches scattered ubiquitously in our neighbourhood whose towers and steeples were to form the familiar landmarks of my childhood. But it was not long before I was taught a little about war and wickedness, rather more about church and churchiness, and much more about the victory of a slain Captain, whose empty tomb in a country far away offered a Day of Remembrance for all nations and promised an eternal country fit "for heroes to live in".

## Ruth's Birthplace

**11 Palace Road, Crouch End, London, now painted white**

# III
# THE "GOOD OLD DAYS"

## Learning "the Truth"

As soon as my legs were strong enough I joined my brother John (who was three and a half years older), together with our parents, to tramp some two miles uphill and down again to the Christadelphian meeting room at Finsbury Park. On our way we passed a number of churches and observed their members wending their several paths. It was good to see them carrying their Bibles, for few of our neighbours stirred from their beds to attend any form of religious service. A census taken at the beginning of the century had indicated that one in every five Londoners went to church or chapel once or twice on a Sunday.[3] But gradually attendance declined, and the Lord's day became for many an opportunity to rest from wearisome weekday work, to read the newspapers and for the more energetic to play tennis, have a day out on the bicycle or, for the well-off, to take a trip in the motor car. But those who did congregate in places of worship attended not because (as often in earlier days) they were obliged to do so by their employers, nor so much for the sake of respectability, but more because they had a desire to worship God. Soon, however, I learned to regard those ladies and gentlemen, dressed just as we were in Sunday-best, with kind but critical eyes. I was told by my mother that though the Wesleyans, in particular, were very good people, yet they, together with all other "churchgoers", were sadly "astray". Their leaders, the clergy, taught falsehoods, for they themselves did not know "the Truth". This "Truth" was taught from the Bible at the meeting. I came to understand that the "Brethren and Sisters" (as the members called each other), as well as those in other Christadelphian meetings,

---

[3] *The Christadelphian*, August 1903, p. 370

11

would care for me better than any other people would ever do.

I remember thinking how privileged I was, for not only did I have loving parents, but I had been born into the midst of the one community which could lead me to everlasting happiness. This sometimes puzzled me but it never occurred to me to question the matter. I knew that other people could be virtuous: my school teachers, my schoolfriends' parents, and then later, a number of colleagues as well as neighbours. But they were not included as God's children because they did not share the same beliefs as Christadelphians. It was unfortunate, but a fact which had to be accepted. And I was taught that Christ's return was imminent and if they were still living, then they would see the error of their beliefs and find a corner, be it ever so little, in the kingdom which Jesus would establish.

During my early infancy an effort was being made among the "ecclesias" (derived from the Greek/Latin word for "church" and which I soon found was an alternative way of describing the meetings) to make special efforts to retain the interest of their young people. Long afterwards I learned of the various suggestions which were discussed. One Brother volunteered that

> ...the managing brethren [the elders] of all Ecclesias should recognize that times are not what they were twenty years ago, that youths and maidens of fifteen to eighteen years of age to-day [1921] are the equal in education and general knowledge to those many years their seniors in past days – consequently, it is necessary that the Ecclesias' treatment or way of handling them in these days should advance with the times, and in this connection we appeal for a deeper, more loving, sympathetic interest being *shown* in them, in their welfare and training.

Another member suggested,

> ...it may be necessary again to deviate from the old-fashioned routine of Ecclesial life, but a change in

this respect would probably be a good thing for all concerned.

The matter was considered of such importance that the Finsbury Park ecclesia convened a special meeting when I was three to discuss remedial action. Nothing under the sun is new, and they were merely struggling with the perennial problem which, as time would pass and education would advance, would became increasingly acute in nearly every community in Christendom.

In the following year, 1924, and in London again, another special meeting was convened. Those summoned to attend were not the Brethren but senior civil servants, representatives of the C.I.D. and of the elementary schools' inspectorate. Their purpose was to discuss "Air Raid Precautions" and plans for the evacuation of children from the potentially more vulnerable areas, plans which would be put into operation should some "unidentified" belligerent ever drop explosives on Britain. Scattered air raids during the Great War (as World War I was then called) had resulted in 1,117 civilian deaths with close to 5,000 injured, and had indicated the loss of life and injuries which any future hostility, aided by the development of aviation and sophisticated missiles, could inflict on the home-front.

While the Christadelphian community and the British government were struggling with the problem of saving their youth, Adolf Hitler, the young dissident and political prisoner who was incarcerated in Landsberg Castle near Munich, was occupying himself with the solution to the problems of the recently defeated and humiliated Germany as he employed himself writing *Mein Kampf* (*My Struggle*). Concurrently those of us in nurseryland (though without nurseries) were becoming familiar with the seemingly jolly little songs which pass down from one generation to another. Blissfully ignorant of any dismal origin or prophetical relevance, we were 'ringing roses' and 'all falling down', and gleefully chanting, "London's burning! London's burning! Fetch the engine! Fetch the engine!...".

On Sundays, however, at the meetings and in the Sunday School I was occupied with more serious considerations. The name "Dr Thomas" was becoming familiar to my ears. I

13

visualised with wonder the famous gentleman who, I understood, had, nearly a hundred years earlier, devoted his life, first in America, to unearthing "the Truth", and then in Britain to preaching his unique message, in contrast to the falsehoods of the churches. It was he who, at the time of the American Civil War had decided on the name "Christadelphian", so forming the community composed of conscientious objectors to national military service, but whose members were not pacifists. They expected that Jesus would soon return and would destroy all his enemies, assisted by the Brethren who were to be established as kings and priests. This community, I learned, was not a church in the usual sense of the word, nor was it a non-conformist body. It was the "sect everywhere spoken against" (Acts 28:22) composed of the "elect" who faithfully followed apostolic doctrine and practice.

The name Robert Roberts, often linked with Dr Thomas, also became familiar to me. He, too, was to be regarded as exceptionally important for he had organised John Thomas' followers into a community. But at home he was spoken of with restrained enthusiasm and gradually I became aware that a big division of the Christadelphians had taken place before I was born, and Finsbury Park meeting was among those who had opposed Robert Roberts. I seem to recall my mother telling me that he was "a hard man". That he and his supporters rejected the admirable members of "our" side was puzzling indeed, but it was a situation which in later years would loom large in my experiences.

It is strange how on reflection in older years we can perceive how odd were some of our childhood conceptions. As I came to know other small children I found that they often referred to their parents as Mummy and Daddy. I thought this very posh for mine were called "Mummer and Dadder". If someone had just explained, once I had learned a little spelling, that I was supposed to be saying "Mamma" and "Dadda", decidedly genteel forms of address, then (absurdly) my self-esteem would have risen. But, anyway, whatever I called them (and as I grew older, they became Mum and Dad), they were held high in my affections – and it's not too late, even now, to correct my spelling?

14

As time went on I became increasingly aware of their dedication to the meetings. Although my father, who was employed as a signal linesman by the London and North Eastern Railway Company, had often to work on Sundays, both he and Mamma attended services as frequently as possible. In their quiet, earnest way, they tried to tell others of their priceless pearl. They were convinced that if any interested "strangers" would only come along to the Sunday evening preaching lectures, and then read for themselves the text-proved "Declaration of the Truth revealed in the Bible as distinguished from the Theology of Christendom", they could not fail to be convinced of the correctness of Christadelphian beliefs and wish to become members.

In our small suburban garden in front of the tall, terraced house, where the large ferns and little golden Jenny Creeper set off the splendour of our whitened doorstep, Dadda erected a sturdy home-made notice board which rose above his neat privet hedge. On it he plastered (with paste made from white flour and water as was our custom) the subject of "the lecture" to be given on the following Sunday evening by one of the highly esteemed "lecturing Brethren". Of course all would be welcome, all seats were free and there would be no collection. This, I thought, was a most acceptable method of letting our neighbours, who so inexplicably ignored "the Truth", realise where it could be found. Not without precedent there could have been added "No annual bazaars" for any such activity, as well as going to concerts and theatres, the "pictures" or circuses, as well as dancing, smoking, and drinking alcohol, were seen as inappropriate for the people of God. It was agreed, as we sang in the hymn, that "While others crowd the house of mirth, and haunt the gaudy show" those who "would with wisdom dwell prefer the house of woe". And as editor Robert Roberts had said in *The Christadelphian* magazine, those who attended theatres and circuses, and any who favoured such a course, could "not have much conception of the requirements of the truth". Even so, some kept the rules more strictly than others, and just occasionally we went to a circus which didn't seem too "gaudy" and I thought was lovely and so clever. But that was long before any serious thought had been given to "animal rights".

# The Sparkhall Family

Ruth's grandparents, Albert and Sarah Sparkhall, with family, in back garden at 11 Palace Road, Crouch End, London, c.1919.

Back *(left to right)*: Doris Sparkhall, Jack Ward, Syd Grantham, Will Cook, Gladys Sparkhall.

Front *(left to right)*: John Ward, May Ward (née Sparkhall), Albert Sparkhall, Sarah Sparkhall (née Hatton), Eunice Cook, Daisy Cook (née Sparkhall), Denis Cook.

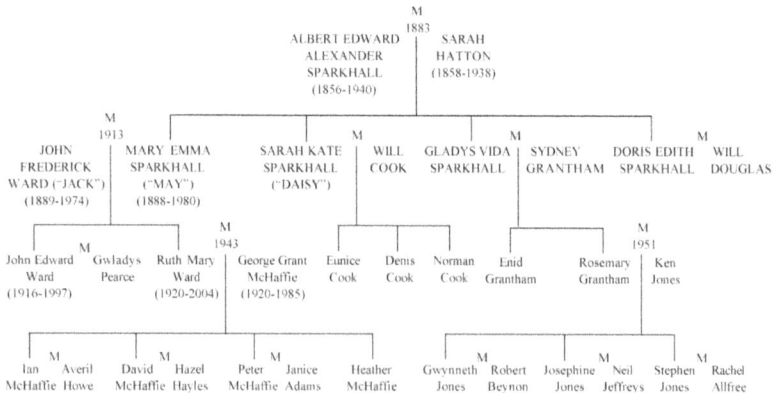

# IV
# HOME TRUTHS

I seldom saw my father's mother, who was not a Christadelphian, and I only remember her as a kind old lady sitting by her fireside, doubtless prematurely aged by rearing, like most of her neighbours, too large a family in deprived circumstances. My apparently irresponsible paternal grandfather had died long before.

Because I spent my childhood in the same house as my maternal grandparents and their youngest daughter, my Auntie Doris, and because they were "Brother and Sister Sparkhall", I knew them much better. Grandad saw himself as a stalwart for "the Truth", and in many ways so he was. He was also a domineering husband and father, though I remember him as being kindly disposed toward me. He was proud that his four daughters, the surviving half of his family, had joined the Christadelphian ranks, though I think they would never have dared to do otherwise. He would have liked them to have sat together in a row in the meeting, but at least by the time I knew them they had taken the liberty of declining. And, anyway, as the older three had soon converted their respective "alien young men" into dedicated Christadelphians, and Auntie Doris later courted and then married a ready-made member, the problem as to who sat with whom was solved to everyone's satisfaction.

Some time later Mamma told me that she never attended the business meetings held from time to time because she was so embarrassed by Grandad's aggressive attitude. He had been greatly annoyed, for example, that the ecclesia had bought some carpeting from an "alien" instead of from his credit-drapery business. But lest it should be thought unkind of me to mention the matter, it must be recalled that his aggression was typical of many Victorian and Edwardian fathers (especially among sectarians, though there were admirable exceptions). It speaks for itself that Charles Walker,

17

when editor of *The Christadelphian* (1899-1937), deliberately ensured that the hymn which commences, "Brethren let us walk together in the bonds of love and peace" was omitted from the hymn book published under his auspices. And his reason was that when it was selected for business meetings, stormy sessions inevitably followed.

When I was born, my maternal Grannie Sparkhall was sixty-one but she always seemed to me to be a frail, lavender-scented old lady in long black or grey clothes, sometimes with a touch of mauve. Adult members of the household had to be at the ready to open her bottle of "sal volatile" (a cardiac stimulant) should she suffer from one of her "turns". It was Grannie who gave me the still-treasured pop-up book which, with her neat writing, she inscribed to "dear little Ruthie". Every reader will understand how easy it was at the age of three to be "dear" to your Grannie when she saw in you something of her four babies who had been laid in the cold earth and for whom, unlike members of the churches in similar circumstances, she could envisage no "home...above the bright blue skies". Only for adults baptised into the same beliefs as Christadelphians was she allowed to believe there could be hope of immortal sainthood, when the earth would be glorified for a thousand years.

Sometimes she would take my hand and lead me up over the dark-brown, bordered strip-lino which covered the stairs to the bedroom she shared with Grandad, and I would admire her feather-stitching on the mauve eiderdown on the bed which, as distinct from my own dark green-painted, iron resting place, had shining brass knobs. On one of her walls I would notice from time to time the coloured print which hung in honour, and which was a picture designed by Dr Thomas, his last work for the Christadelphian community. I never really understood its meaning but the lovely "white" Jesus, with his golden hair falling to his shoulders, and his standing on top of the globe beside an amiable lion, with Moses on his right hand and John the Baptist on his left, and with a neatly designed Cross beneath, all seemed to fit in admirably with my gentle infant milieu. And whatever grandeur we lacked, that picture encapsulated the love and security which surrounded my early days, and the contentment I enjoyed both at home and at the meeting.

As I was a child of Christadelphians it is surprising that for the first six years of my education I attended an Anglican church school. But desirable though my parents thought the exclusive "Elm House" at the end of the road with its well-mannered, uniformed girls in purple, since we were unable to afford fees, it was decided that "Holy Innocents", with the high church tower standing close by, would offer me a gentler environment than John had encountered at the (by then so-called) Board school. In many areas in England and Wales teachers were having to cope with some fifty to sixty pupils in their classes, and, though in London numbers were lower, even there infants numbered up to forty-six. But at Holy Innocents there were only around thirty in each of the three classes, though two classes shared one room which must have been distracting for the teachers – since it offered alternative listening for the pupils.

Gentle though I found the new environment, there were no preliminary introductions for newcomers and it was a nine-to-four day from the very beginning. But we had a long "dinner time", twelve till two if I remember correctly, and no school dinners, so at least there was a welcome respite in between the sessions, and on return in the afternoon we complied with Miss Taylor's instruction that we should have a little rest with heads cushioned by folded arms on our tables. But since I had never been parted from my mother before, the "babies' class" enclosed in a room with high narrow windows seemed to me like prison, and it was a tearful experience despite dear Miss Taylor sitting me in her lap. Most of my peers seem to have been much braver as they faced the new experience. It was not to be the only occasion in life when I would observe other people finding more courage than I. It was, I suppose, the first time that I discovered that whatever for each of us are "green pastures", we do not stay in them "forever", and that there are the many changing scenes of life to be faced when we have no choice but to soldier on. But although I was too young to see "the rainbow through rain" yet somehow the card proclaiming "a" for a beautiful apple which, together with its twenty-five associates, hung on the wall, gained my attention and set me on the road to the compulsory and free education which, as compared with earlier generations, I was (unknowingly) so privileged to receive.

Before long I would learn in "drawing" that I was not to depict on paper what I *thought* was there but only what I could see. And so the still-life carrot, bereft of its foliage, and which faced me "head-on", appeared in my approved masterpiece looking like one of the polo mints which in later years would decorate the sweet-shop counters. But, more importantly as time went on, I would learn at the meeting that "what is seen is temporary, but what is unseen is eternal", and it was on the latter, not on the former, that those of us who were wise would "fix our eyes".

Despite my parents' exclusive doctrinal convictions, apparently they had no objections to my participating in any of the religious activities in the "infants", so I was soon playing a full part in the curriculum and finding that school wasn't so bad after all. May Day celebrations might have been inaugurated by the Druids, and the Puritans of the seventeenth century had taken exception to the jollity which came to be associated with it. But I suppose Mamma and Dadda felt it was harmless enough for little ones to be decked with flowers, to have a child selected as the "May Queen" and to rejoice at the return of summer's beauty. And to me that all seemed a wonderful idea.

Empire Day followed on the 24th of the same month, the anniversary of Queen Victoria's birthday. Though England today apparently pays little attention to it, the inhabitants of Edinburgh (in which city I have now lived for over fifty years) wishing, I suppose, to show Scotland's united, unwavering loyalty to the Crown, still celebrate her birthday with a holiday on the Monday nearest to the 24th. After all, it was Victoria who helped to make Scotland special. In my infancy and on Empire Day, flags, large and small, were waved throughout Britain, the Union Jack symbolising the Empire which embraced a fifth of the world's surface and which was held so triumphantly. And I waved my flag too.

"And I waved my flag too."

Christadelphians were as jubilant at Britain's prowess and possession of her colonies as was everyone else, for it was believed that the British Empire had a tremendously important part to play when Jesus Christ returned at the time of "the End". Represented, as was believed, by "the merchants of Tarshish and all the young lions thereof" referred to in the Bible, she would help Christ to subdue all his enemies, and in particular "the king of the north" (presumed to be Russia). After that enormous victory, the reigning monarch, by then George V, would lay the British crown at Jesus' feet. It had been hoped that Queen Victoria, symbolised by the Queen of Sheba, would play that role. But as John Carter would point out, when as editor of *The Christadelphian* magazine he republished (in 1940) Dr Thomas' 1866 pamphlet *The Destiny of the British Empire*, the sex of the monarch was not important. And so, all in all, it was appropriate for me to join with other children in Empire Day celebrations, for Britannia had the largest maritime force in the world. She did indeed "rule the waves," and the Britons 'never, never, never would be slaves'.

The Christadelphians harboured strongly disapproving feelings about the annual Remembrance Day. John Thomas had emphasised at a meeting held by pacifists that war was all part of God's plan, and no attempt should be made to prevent it. There was never any question of the Brethren and Sisters remembering "the glorious dead" or praying for peace (other than for peace after Armageddon). But I was allowed, like the other children, to buy a penny poppy. Following the pattern of America and then France, in 1921 the British war disabled were employed to make the poppies, the silk variety for those who could afford to pay more and cotton ones for the rest of us. They were sold mostly by genteel ladies in the streets, and the proceeds helped those who had survived or half survived the latest major effort of the nation to preserve the Empire. And none would have dared (Christadelphians included unless at a meeting), whether in school, the workshop, the street or in any public place, to do anything other than breathe and think during the two minutes' silence observed at 11 a.m. on 11th November each year.

There were no "parents' evenings" in my schooldays, and communication between school and home was limited. The only notes which were written by teachers (other than in exceptional circumstances) were brief reports on progress, and those only in later years. Children are not particularly adept at reporting information correctly which results in misunderstandings. I must have been worse than most. When a play (presumably of the nativity variety) was put on by the infant performers, I was to be an angel. When mothers were invited to attend the afternoon performance (few, if any, fathers could take time off work) mine was distressed to discover that my fellow angels had discarded their woolly jumpers etc and were in ethereal dress. However, all was not lost, for overnight an "in stock" remnant of blue material with gold threads running through it, was run up on the sewing machine, and I was transformed at the repeat performance on next day – outwardly, at least. Perhaps dress made not only "the man" but also the angel?

Although during that infant stage of my education I was allowed to stay with my peers for Bible stories, when at Christmas time I returned home singing merrily, "We three kings of Ori an' Are...", Dadda, though a most reluctant correspondent owing to his skeletal education, felt obliged to write to my teacher to check the wording. Whether this was to satisfy his curiosity or to prevent my imbibing a theological error I cannot now recall.

"On the way home from school"

# V
# MOVING UP

When I was eight I moved up to St Mary's Girls' school where, by parental request, I was excused from Scripture lessons and from the school's occasional attendance at the Parish Church. These withdrawals were in line with the caution given by Robert Roberts in *The Ambassador* (1868), and were intended to prevent "that powerful inoculation of error which takes place in a young mind among large numbers in circumstances of respectability".[4]

By now I had discovered that Christadelphians used vocabulary which was either unknown to my schoolfriends or used differently. My playmates never talked about the "Brethren and Sisters", nor about "fraternal gatherings", the "memorial service" nor even "the Truth". But I soon learned to adapt my wording to whichever company I was in, and I was old enough and enthusiastic enough to know that it was good to stand up for Jesus. I was eager to explain to friend Joan something of our unique beliefs. On the way home from school, and near the old wall in Rokesely Avenue which supplied us with mini ferns to 'fernish' our mini gardens, I announced what I thought to be the first principle, "We don't believe in going to heaven when you die". My theology was perhaps more carefully constructed than my grammar, and whether or not Joan divulged that information to her parents I don't know. But either way, she remained my "best friend", and our minds concentrated seriously, and mostly, on the welfare and continuous survival of our beloved papier-maché dollies, suffering grievous distress when bathing one of them resulted in unforeseen disaster.

---

[4] *The Ambassador of the Coming Age* (later *The Christadelphian*), February 1868, p. 53

The people in the meeting lived up to everything my parents led me to expect. They were genuinely concerned for "Ruthie", with the smiling Sisters going out of their way to include her in their conversations and greet her with their kisses. I looked admiringly at the flowing, flowery georgette and charming pastel crepe-de-chine frocks with large matching hats which some could afford. To become like one of those sweet and beautiful ladies when I grew up was my heart's desire. But alas! Such elegance and style were never to be mine for as one Sister told me later "...you look so insignificant". But I did have one little "pretence" when I was fifteen and Auntie Doris invited me to be her bridesmaid. By way of complementing Auntie's beautiful, beige velvet gown, Mamma made me a long, "crushed strawberry" taffeta dress which was accompanied by one of the latest petal hats, together with a posy assembled from Dadda's everlasting flowers (for free). Principle forbade the ceremony to be held in a church, and, as yet, the meeting had no licensed hall, so the wedding was in a registry office (with never so much as a photo of bride and groom). Afterwards I just went back home and became "normal" again, but it was a brief moment of elegance, and, of course, even more so for Auntie.

After her marriage, Sunday mornings were never quite the same, for previously my Uncle-to-be used to call for her on his way to the meeting. While Auntie powdered her nose (shiny ones were not in fashion and young sisters liked to be fashionable) and made herself "just so", Uncle played the pedal organ in Grannie's "best room", and I was delighted to warble along, free to choose my favourite hymns. "When summer suns are glowing" (the musical setting, unknown to me, but suitably entitled "Ruth") was first in my top ten. But I had no understanding that for many in the world the "summer suns" of life were never glowing, and that multitudes never experienced "God's free mercy streaming...".

Some might conclude that during my childhood I was being indoctrinated into Christadelphianism. If that was so then it was in the kindest of ways both at home and in the ecclesia. I was never aware of being pressurised, though critics might argue that my unawareness was all part of the process.

But that the motive of my parents and the Brethren and Sisters was entirely good as they followed the biblical instruction to bring up a child in the way "he" should go, is not to be questioned.

Expectations of parents from their children and expectations of children from their parents were then on a different level from today. From the time of my earliest memory I always knew that above every other wish it was hoped that I would grow up to "be a good girl" as my mother described the prospect of my being baptised by immersion into the Christadelphian faith. Though the hopes of parents in the community today still have a spiritual dimension yet most are anxious that the secular education of their children will ensure that they are among the front-runners in the rat-race (however ugly we find that expression). That our "youths and maidens" (equally) should become sufficiently qualified to gain positions in one or other of the well-paid sectors of our competitive society is a high priority. All of which helps to make us a relatively affluent community, and no longer working class. Perhaps it is true to say that for Christian parents to find the right balance between the spiritual and the material, the things which are seen and the things which are not, grows increasingly difficult.

In contrast to my early years, many children of "ordinary" parents today expect from them not only love and attention but also expensive gear and extravagant gifts. Additionally, many see it as an essential ingredient of life that they speed "to and fro", passing the driving test at the earliest opportunity and taking possession of the family car as often as possible, or better still, being sufficiently well-financed to acquire one of their own. While our grandchildren have toured Europe, the States or the (formerly) remote parts of the world either with their parents, school parties or independently, my own ambition to explore new fields stopped short at sallying forth with my parents to find a bluebell wood. I used to watch "big boys" on their bikes riding through the streets carrying home huge bunches of (wilting) bluebells, and couldn't imagine where such splendour could be found. But Dadda, when working "down the line" (I think at South or North Mimms) managed eventually to espy a wood, carpeted with blue – and, oh what delight when at last we took a trip on a train and were able to walk in wonderland!

Whether today's advantages and experiences make for better people than those reared in the nineteen-twenties and thirties is debatable. But it is, I think, true to say that up-dated education, with all its opportunities and the encouragement given to children to form independent opinions, makes for a more sympathetic understanding of the problems of others and a less condemnatory attitude toward those who are disadvantaged or who differ from themselves. While modern education has resulted in our community's loss of many young people, now known as "teenagers", yet today, perhaps as never before, there is a large proportion of the Christadelphian young working in the caring professions, even though that involves Sunday work which, in earlier days, they were advised to avoid.

# VI
# DAY BY DAY
# AND WEEK BY WEEK

## 'Homes fit for Heroes'

Although after the 1914-18 Great War it was intended that there would be "homes fit for heroes", in fact, there was a housing shortage five times greater than the pre-war level. Many working class families living in rooms had to share just about everything – including the one lavatory – outside the back door or on the landing. Running water (cold) was available from outside communal taps. Though cleanliness might have been next to Godliness, neither was achieved without a struggle, and it was easy for people to be smelly, though, as always, some did better than others whatever the circumstances. Slums stretched extensively throughout Britain with some living in houses condemned since the middle of the previous century. Glasgow, even today having more deprivation than elsewhere in Britain, topped the list with nearly 200,000 people living more than three to a room. When council houses were built in the 1920s the rents were higher than ordinary people could afford, and the homes were inspected to ensure that they were kept clean with no fleas or whatever lurking in the beds. Tenants knew nothing of "human rights".

From the beginning of their married lives, my parents occupied rented accommodation. They were well situated by comparison with many for they shared a house not with just anyone, but only with Grannie and Grandad, and Mamma's unmarried sisters. Before I was born, the family had moved to a quite spacious domain at number 11 Palace Road with its two long flights of stairs alternating with two small ones. In the winter, gas lighting illuminated the hallway on the groundfloor (and the large antlers on the wall) but did little to help the top flight. So the spookiness together with the

29

absence of heating ensured that it was negotiated as quickly as possible. At least the large kitchen was warm, equipped as it was with a big black-leaded range and with a curtain-skirted dresser where I could hide. An adjacent scullery provided a shallow, yellow stone sink, a once-a-week coal-fired copper and an iron mangle with its wooden rollers ("Watch your fingers!"). To my then uncritical eyes it seemed to be in reasonable condition but had seen better days. The pull bells to summon the maid(s) were still in situ, and that they didn't ring caused no inconvenience.

My first memory of sleeping arrangements is that my bed was beside Mamma's and Dadda's while John slept over by the window. Later he was given a little room of his own and I stayed put until I was "too big", whereupon Auntie Doris welcomed me into her room. We were among the fortunates for, unlike so many others, we had a family bathroom with a lavatory ("toilet" and the later "loo" not, as yet, part of the vocabulary). There was even an outside lavatory, so we were well "convenienced". Many years later, I was appalled to recall that we were so far "downstairs" that newspaper or tissues which had wrapped our tangerines (the forerunners of mandarins and clementines) were used for toilet paper. But now that TV has revealed all and we can discuss anything and everything, I find that the same experience was shared by my lady-like elderly friends, some of whom were in better financial circumstances than we were.

The old range supplied enough hot water for each of us to have the luxury of an individual bath once a week. In winter the shiveringly low temperatures were raised by the "Valor Perfection" paraffin oil stove, lit (at least for me) specially for the occasions. Dadda, during my early years, supplemented his bathing by breaking the ice on the New River reservoir(s) and having a swim which apparently was permissible and also enjoyable before his day of working on the signals/rails.

Our landlord was not overkeen (perhaps of his own necessity) to improve the decor of the house. But my mother liked to keep everything "nice" even if lacking in grandeur. When, however, she attempted to clean the high, distempered (white-washed) ceiling in our best ("front") room which had become sooted by the gas lighting, she made a patchy mess.

30

Though her effort proved disastrous and we learned that some things really don't wash, we also learned that good marks, which Dadda was always ready to give to Mamma, could be awarded for trying.

And all was forgotten when to our delight Mr Dearing, the landlord, had the room re-decorated, and we were allowed to choose the wallpaper, provided we didn't select one of the "dearer" varieties. We chose with such care and enthusiasm that I still see the pink, leafy pattern weaving its way round the walls.

"Mamma liked to keep everything nice."

Crouch End neighbourhood was quiet and apparently respectable, with any domestic turmoils kept hush-hush. Divorce was considered disreputable by most people and any unmarried mothers, if they were seen, were expected to remain unheard, and were even sent long-term to mental institutions. I was only vaguely aware that there was something "funny" about the neighbours to one side of us. And whatever the cause, obviously little Douglas had never been taught the Fourth Commandment. Leaning over the garden wall and watching my father at work, he called out one day, "You're clever. My Dad ain't!". Miss Simpson, living on the other side, together with her grand piano, was select and intelligent. But even she was "astray", at least in a kindly way, being unique, so I thought, in believing it wrong to kill anything since "it" might once have been a person, or might in the future become one. How she coped with the summer invasion of London house-flies without any of those abominable fly-papers I can't imagine, though, admittedly, there was some difficulty in deciding whether the flies were more acceptable alive than trapped in a sticky mess hanging on a strip above our heads. As one of the privileged class (an owner-occupier) she was able to let her ground-floor rooms to Mr and Mrs Vinall. While Dadda went to "work", Mr Vinall, a white-collared worker, went to "business". And they must have been "well-off" for their small daughter annually received exquisitely decorated Easter eggs. John and I were given only plain ones (extra "plain", for if I remember correctly, no "milk" chocolate eggs were made – at least not for the hoi polloi market). But their plainness seemed like "the Truth", and were appreciated every bit as much.

Thanks to the work of social reformers, often dedicated members of the "alien" churches, the stark deprivation suffered in the Victorian and Edwardian eras was, by the time of my childhood, somewhat alleviated. But life for the lower classes was still hard. Welfare provision was meagre with unemployment rife. For those in work, wages were so low that it was difficult to build up any reserve, and those who lost their jobs were expected to use up any money they had saved, and sell any furniture which the authorities deemed "unnecessary", albeit their only soft chair.

In the early years of the 19th century "friendly societies" had been inaugurated informally in public houses. Dissenting churches had seen the need for regular organisation of these clubs so as to give them respectability and their removal to more desirable premises. A society would be formed and officers elected, and the groups allowed the occasional use of a schoolroom for meetings, together with a supply of candles as necessary. Each member had to subscribe a regular small amount to obtain benefit during illness and medical attention, and a payment was made at the death of one in the family (a frequent occurrence).

By the time of my infancy the societies were well established and the poor were able to make at least some provision for rainy days. The more prudent, who could manage to squeeze out a few pennies weekly, availed themselves of the opportunity. From the age of 6 months I was insured at a ha'penny a week against funeral expenses, which, with hindsight, was a dreadful waste of badly needed half pennies. The "insurance man" called regularly to collect the family contributions and to make sure that they were kept up to date, as of course they were. Christadelphians could "do no other".

The Brotherhood did its best to help those in financial distress, more particularly among its own – and the Jews, "God's chosen people". Parents in those days were likely to die young and the "Orphan Fund" aided the community's children. In some meetings (and only in some) there was the occasional collection for "outsiders". For Mamma and Dadda, keeping up with even modest household requirements meant screwing and scraping, making-do and mending. But everything was paid for "on the dot", for they followed the scriptural injunction "Owe no man anything...". They bought what they could afford and did without any item they couldn't. "Hire Purchase" (the "never-never") which had been introduced around the turn of the century was frowned upon by the respectable even in the world, and respectability was exceptionally important. Foolhardy customers who contemplated so reckless a method of purchase were encouraged on the way to ruin by the retailers' willingness to deliver in plain vans, circumventing any critical neighbourhood watch.

My mother was the only one of her sisters whose husband never suffered the misfortune of falling out of work. This meant that John and I had an undisturbed existence as compared with our cousins. Our better-educated Uncle Syd Grantham was for some years in a "good" job. It was he who could afford a camera and he was almost entirely responsible for our collection of early family photos. But when I was about twelve, he opened a fruiterer's shop. Unfortunately sales were too low and the business had to close. As a result, the extended family eventually came to the rescue and shared accommodation. We in "Palace Road" squeezed up so that Auntie and Uncle with baby Rosemary could move in, joined by Enid after she had spent about a year with Auntie Daisy, Uncle Will Cook and family. A makeshift kitchen with a gas cooker was assembled on the top landing (with running water and lavatory three flights down). It must have been horribly inconvenient, but for Enid and me it brought some especially happy years of close companionship, with the added delight of the resident toddler.

## Rags, bones – and rubbish

As well as road sweepers it was commonplace to see men and boys wheeling barrows, used for a variety of purposes. From time to time the rag and bone man circulated the neighbourhood, collecting items which could be recycled. Woollen articles would make suits and coats of "shoddy" for the lower end of the market. Had we added to his collection I would have been given a balloon in exchange. But what today would be "rags" were not rags then. Sheets wearing thin in the middle would be "turned" and Mamma would machine them up so that the less worn areas were replaced by the thicker edges, and they would end their days made into babies' cot sheets, linings for washable nappies or washable sanitary towels (the only variety she knew, as also I and my contemporaries for many years). Cuffs and collars, other than the detachable stiff collars which Dadda wore for best and which every "white-collared" gentleman wore regularly, would be reversed so that the worn side was not visible. Eventually our cast-off clothing was valuable as dusters and "floor cloths". And I think we never bought enough meat to have sufficient bones to add to the barrow collection, so I never received any of the balloons. But it didn't matter – for we knew that, very soon, it was the rich who would be sent empty away, and balloons (at least of a spiritual nature) would be given in abundance to the children of the elect for "they [the children] are holy".

The dustman called every week, tramping through the house to the back garden, heaving the big galvanised bin on to his back, carrying it to the dust-cart in the road and returning it empty to the back garden. A miserable job and miserly wages, but it was a job – and in those times few could afford to argue about working conditions nor any (as yet unheard of) "job descriptions".

## From Day to Day

The milkman, with his horse and cart, delivered early every morning, waking sleepy-heads as the glass empties were clattered together for return to the dairy. Mr Hinds, the baker, arrived too, sometimes giving John and me a short ride along the road. And as we trotted back we thought it appropriate (only once I hope) to gather London Pride out of neighbours' gardens. After all, didn't God make "each little flower that opens" for everyone? And didn't Dadda take great pride in being one of His London helpers? With John I could be brave – but what about all those Sunday School lessons?

My father's enthusiasm for tilling the soil (despite battling with "thorns and thistles") was a valuable asset to home economy. Our back garden, though only a small area, provided enough room to grow some vegetables (especially runner beans) as well as flowers, and room for the workshed he built from whatever bits of wood he could acquire, not forgetting the invaluable orange boxes available from greengrocers. From his allotment near the railwaymen's hut (with Alexandra Palace towering majestically nearby), the sweetest scented spring onions, pinks and chrysanthemums were hauled home on his bike.

35

It seems a long while ago, now, since any Brother would appear at the meeting on a Sunday morning with a prized bloom filling his button-hole (preferably in a metal container of water hidden beneath his lapel). But Dadda's floral decoration drew great appreciation. Inter alia, habits have changed. Button-holes are now empty except at those grand weddings when expensive exotic flowers (largely flown in from abroad and then undreamed of) are plentiful. We had our "bunches" of course, but florists' formal arrangements were, so far as we were concerned, more for funerals than anything else. "Interflora" had only recently blossomed forth, and we would have been neither senders nor recipients. Come to think of it – a funny word "button-hole" – for it is either the hole or the flower arrangement that fills it. Just an example, perhaps, of a word which had it been in the Bible could have caused endless argument, and even division among those who so often claim to be united in Christ but never seem to be so for long. Obviously interpreting languages correctly needs more than a knowledge of vocabulary.

There is a wonder in childhood which, happily, for the poor, compensates for lack of luxury and adds its own joy, but sadly fades as we grow older and perceptions change. There must be others who, like myself, now see convolvulus as a pernicious weed needing instant eradication, but who once saw it displaying the beauty of a white lily (which it does). There must be others, too, who can remember perhaps a cluster of cherry blossom blown from a neighbour's tree and gleefully gathered up, or a rosebud dropped by a passer-by, causing a serious debate as to which of the two finders was to have the privilege of keeping it. But how good it is that despite our modern sophistication, there are still little ones who, like the infants when escorted to the park for their school sports, wanted to pick daises instead of running races, or the toddler who was so delighted with the one flower she acquired from the bride's bouquet! And how appropriate it was that Jesus "called a little child, set him in their midst" and told his disciples, "I tell you the truth, unless you change and become like little children you will never enter the kingdom of heaven".

Shopping occupied much of Mamma's time for almost all our requirements had to be carried home – and Grannie's, too. The alluring penny bazaar (Marks and Spencer in its infancy), and Woolworths stores (imported from America) were beginning to proliferate in London, the latter selling "nothing over sixpence". And there was the Caledonian Cattle Market which (on non-marketing days and in the absence of cattle) displayed a tantalising display of cheap goods loudly touted by the persuasive stall-holders, and provided a special "afternoon out". The local Co-op was, of necessity, specially favoured. At the time of purchase, Mamma gave her Co-op share number in order to gain dividends. The magic 104049 still springs more readily to mind than my phone number (an experience familiar to many contemporaries). On the eagerly awaited "divi day" she would receive back two shillings and sixpence (twelve and a half per cent) for every pound spent, though the divi rate varied in keeping with trade. Some Christadelphians wondered whether any in the Brotherhood should hold so worldly a membership, and those with small businesses saw the Co-ops and Woolworths as menacing rivals, but there was general approval – which was just as well for the likes of us. "Divi day" was a meaningful event, not just a frill – and the Co-op was a meaningful organisation for it was effective in improving working and housing conditions and much else besides. It is still socially conscious today with its "Fair Trade" products helping to prevent the exploitation of the growers of tea, coffee and chocolate beans, and offering visa cards which benefit Oxfam and Amnesty International. Mrs Fry, one of their volunteer workers, ran an evening play-centre to which I was introduced. But only home and "meeting" activities were to my liking, and my attendance was short-lived.

Perhaps because of my close proximity to them I have clear recollections of shop floors. The butchers (all the butchers I think) had their floors covered with sawdust which caught the blood dripping from the huge carcasses suspended from above. Sainsbury's, which seemed big to me but was only a small shop, had a most attractive all-over mosaic. It was Sainsbury's who, in 1950 would open Britain's first self-service store – in Croydon, and it was left to the St. Cuthbert's

Co-op in Edinburgh to open Scotland's first-ever supermarket in 1955.

In Wilson's, the select local departmental store in Crouch End where genteel ladies enjoyed their dainty afternoon delicacies in the tea-room, it was not so much the shop floor but the overhead wires which attracted my attention. I perched on one of the high bentwood chairs – usefully provided here and there beside the counters for the comfort of weary shoppers or small children. Cash taken by the shop assistant was put into a little container and whizzed along the wire to the cashier, who whizzed back the change. Auntie Doris, who was employed by the "United Dairies" in the exacting task of keeping account of payments collected by the milkmen on their rounds, had earlier been on the staff in the counting house at Wilson's. When she left school at fourteen Grandad had approached the management and gained her a "position". Above the shop premises was accommodation for the young lady employees (a common arrangement). Auntie, being local, lived at home but she would hear the adventures of those who lived-in, and the severe reprimand they received when the supervisor found some of them acting "Delilah" on the beds. What was deemed appalling behaviour in the early 20th century would pass unnoticed today!

Despite earlier reforms, many women during my early days were exploited in mills and factories with low wages and appalling conditions. Even so, they preferred the sociability and the team spirit which they found there rather than being imprisoned as the parlour or scullery maid by some fractious, demanding mistress in a private house, as many of their mothers had been. In rural areas where we liked to imagine everything was so idyllic, the working and living conditions were just as bad for parents and children alike. Young Irish girls unable to find employment would cross the Irish Sea, glad to find work whatever the conditions. A contemporary devout Catholic has described to me the harsh conditions and the miserable shack accommodation they shared when they came "tattie-howking" – gathering up potatoes in Scottish fields, their knees bleeding with the constant kneeling. And yet, after the many tribulations which later life brought to her, she looked back and remembered the good times and the happy comradeship which, while feeling far from home, the workers had together. Meanwhile new technology was gradually making its way into factories. The conveyor-belt system had been introduced earlier in North America, when a pig could go into the meat factory alive and then speedily reappear, sanitised as pork, ready for the consumer. The new system replaced piece-work, and soon mass-produced motor cars, electrical goods and wirelesses were rolling off the assembly lines as well as dismembered animals. For some the new system brought higher wages if they could cope with the pressure of speed, but for others, lower. In 1932 women in the Lucas factory, where work on the even more productive system was based on time and motion studies, were collapsing under the strain of the speed demanded. But shop workers enjoyed no better conditions – with fifty-six hour weeks in boot and shoe retailers, seventy-five hour weeks in bakers and even longer in corner shops. Even nurses in the mid-1930s were putting in between fifty and sixty hours a week for miserly reward. Waitresses in the popular teashops were cruelly exploited. Employed in the flourishing Lyons catering firm, some were committing suicide rather than endure the long hours and stingy wages that left them starving. The staff were warned against informing prospective employees, a number of them Irish, of the conditions which awaited them in England's grand capital.

Although Dadda's income was low there was never any question of my mother going out to work. He would have felt it a disgrace that he was not providing for her, John and me. And that was the usual pattern for those counting themselves respectable and socially above the lower working classes, whether they were in the meeting or not. Nor would my father (on grounds of conscience) ever seek Sunday work, as many of his workmates did, to supplement the low pay. At home we couldn't afford the labour-saving devices, such as the vacuum cleaner and electric cooker, which the better-off were acquiring, together with a "daily" charwoman, so as to overcome the shortage of live-in maids after the Great War. In any case, we had no electricity to feed the new appliances, and a gas cooker would have been an absurd waste. Coal was heaved by the blackened coalman through the round hole (with its iron plate removed) just outside the front door, down into the long, dark cellar. It gave us warmth from the range, hot water in the taps, with the kettle simmering on top, boiling facilities for small loads of washing in an enamel bowl, cooking in the heavy iron saucepans, heating for the flat iron and Mamma's rudimentary hair curlers, splendid toast and a good oven as well as drying facilities overhead. What more could we want? The sturdy wooden Bissell (carpet sweeper), pushed along by Mum's own steam, and her elbow grease kept everything in order. We had a limited choice of cleansing agents, and none of the "wonder-working" detergents or polishes of today. Soda dissolved in hot water was the vital cleaner for the tough jobs.

Early on Monday mornings the fire under the large stone copper in the scullery had to be lit. Rinso washing powder and large double bars of yellow Sunlight soap were indispensable. The "whites" were improved with a "dolly" (a small muslin bag which added a touch of blue to the rinsing water) before the articles were hauled across the stone floor to be wrung through the mangle and then hung on the kitchen pulleys. The weekly pattern was observed without fail. When I came home for dinner on Mondays the kitchen was damp and steamy and it seems we always had stew, often with dumplings. Good it was, too.

I never remember Dadda helping with washing-up or making meals. And few of his contemporaries ever did. When the breadwinner had to work long hours often in back-breaking conditions, a self-respecting wife would never have expected that he should do any housework. But as a dutiful husband, my father played an invaluable role not only in bringing home the pay packet and allotment vegetables, but also in doing a wide variety of mending jobs. It was no throw-away society but one which demanded that the working classes be schooled in "waste not, want not" perhaps more than in anything else. If broken items could be mended then mended they had to be, and if it were possible to extend the life of our possessions by taking care, then take care we did. Dadda put rubber soles and circular rubber heels on new shoes, and would replace them when they became worn, while the boots worn by John (and other boys as well as my father) were reinforced with metal blakeys to withstand hard wear. Broken china was not automatically put in the dustbin. Uncle Dick, Dadda's brother, who earned his living as a china riveter until his eyesight failed, could come to the rescue if we had a mishap with any of the "best" articles. That the mended plate or whatever looked as though it were held together by extra strong paper "staples" provided an excellent example of careful handiwork and household economy.

## Time to Celebrate

Poverty is always relative, and although I knew that we had to spend carefully I never thought we were poor. By comparison with today's standards we, together with most of our friends, were decidedly so. Life's high spots were necessarily celebrated in low-key – of necessity as much as of principle. But that doesn't mean we didn't enjoy ourselves. We looked forward eagerly to Christmases and birthdays, and both rose to expectations.

Though some Christadelphians regarded (and still regard) Christmas as a merely pagan festival that should not be celebrated by true Christians, I was unaware of the fact. That the "Scotch", with their heritage of John Knox's stern Calvinism, habitually went to their places of work as usual on Christmas Day would have appalled me. But I was not much interested in their way of life in the back of beyond, and never dreamed that they would ever play any part in my personal affairs, secure as I was, firmly rooted in "Merrie England".

As the festive event approached Dadda brought home a turkey which he plucked, smothering the kitchen with feathers. Come Christmas Day, grandparents, cousins, aunties, 'uncle Tom Cobley and all' squeezed into the kitchen for the dinner of the year. Afterward we went upstairs to the "front room" – and some years we had a Christmas tree with wax candles perched perilously in tin holders, and a fairy (only hopefully fireproof) hovering at the top. A lucky dip from a tub made an excellent and cheaper alternative, though naturally (or rather spiritually) I was given to understand at an early age that we didn't believe in luck any more than we

41

believed in fairies (who were not to be confused with angels as small girls sometimes did and even yet still do).

That our presents were wrapped in second-time-around, creased, brown paper seemed altogether acceptable as did our garish, joyfully stuck together, home-made chains. And though the only tinsel then available tarnished quickly, the memories it left behind did not. Never can I forget Grandad's annual recitations, "The boy stood on the burning deck...", and "Father is late, said the watching boy...". We all listened with grave attention and suitably respectful admiration – at least I thought we did, but (then unknown to me) there was suppressed mirth among members of the family a few years my senior who, unseen, huddled together behind the couch.

Birthdays were celebrated on much the same level as at Christmas. I don't remember ever having a birthday cake, but the pink and white ha'penny meringues (with no cream but lots of giggles) shared with friend Joan and her little sister were equally enjoyable. And what could have been more acceptable than a few high gloss, birthday postcards, so often decorated with brightly coloured pansies, and delivered by the dapper, distinctive peak-capped postman for a penny? Presents were cheap and modest – perhaps a doll from the Caledonian Market, a pencil box or one containing hard and (for small children) not very effective squares of water paints, a little box of rainbow wool with wooden knitting needles, maybe a book or other small articles. And could the high-tech gifts showered upon children today rise to the "programmed" magic incorporated in a bunch of scented, pheasant-eye narcissi, or a little posy of the sweet violets then cultivated commercially in Cornwall and Devon, and transported daily by rail to the capital? But it was luxury indeed when Joan's parents rose magnificently to buying her a "fairy cycle" – which kept us out of harm's way as we gleefully learned to ride – always restricted to her short garden path.

## Satisfying Appetites – Natural and Spiritual

With most incomes strictly limited, plain, filling dishes were the order of the day. Rice, macaroni, semolina and tapioca, with blancmange or jelly turned out of fancy moulds for special treats, were important ingredients of our diet. Quiches and pizzas, Continental, Eastern and Indian foods, and restaurants providing them, did not put in appearance until well after World War II. Fish and chip shops were the only "carry-outs" and were very popular, supplying, as they did, cheap and nutritious food – plonked on to thin grease-proof paper, with newspaper always used for the outside wrapping. But our own were fried at home. As a family we never had a "meal out" other than a picnic. It seemed an enormous treat when my biology mistress took me for tea at the grand Lyons Corner House in the Strand. There we were served by the immaculate, dapper waitresses, the "nippies" – both of us unaware of their outrageous conditions of employment.

Even had we, as a family, been able to afford to eat out we wouldn't have wanted to, for in common with almost all public places, whether during work or leisure hours, the atmosphere was murky blue, thick with tobacco smoke – usually, by the 1920s, from cigarettes rather than pipes. Only "health fanatics" and some of the more puritanical sects eschewed the habit. Health warnings were seldom heard and the danger of "passive" smoking was unrecognised. Many smokers grew thin and emaciated as their years passed, while the cigarette manufacturers grew fat. Even when travelling by train few of the carriages were "non-smokers", and if occupying one of those we were likely to be embarrassed by the request, "Do you mind if I smoke?". If we registered an objection, even politely, the atmosphere, though smoke-free, was likely to become frosty. We, at school in the 1930s, eagerly collected and swapped the attractive cigarette cards, one given free in each packet. Getting a complete series was difficult if your father didn't smoke (few mothers did) but clean, newly discarded empty packets could be found on the streets and were searched eagerly. One of the leading tobacconists, Players, produced a set (50, I think) of beautifully coloured butterflies – and the "Blue Turquoise" (Number 40?) was hard to find and therefore greatly prized.

We could buy some imported fruits and vegetables – oranges, grapes, bananas and onions (the last of these often carried from door to door slung on poles on the backs of

French pedlars), but there was none of the huge variety on display today. Tomatoes and cucumbers were only to be found in the greengrocers in season, and we eagerly bought a two-inch portion of cucumber when they appeared in the summer. A cucumber sandwich was a luxury (and, as old habits die hard, I still think it is). We heard nothing of "organic" foods because industrialised farming with chemical fertilisers and the use of insecticides were still some thirty years in the future. Strawberries, too, were available only in the summer but when they did arrive in the shops they had none of the bullet-like texture and insipidity which often accompany the imported, chemically-boosted varieties flown into the country today. Home freezers and speedy, modern transport have added variety to our diets and floral arrangements, but they have taken away the anticipation and the pleasure of eating "in season", as well as the scents associated distinctively with each spring, summer, winter and autumn.

The first frozen food (asparagus) did not come on to the market in Britain until I was seventeen, and was unknown to me – it was too expensive a luxury. Fresh asparagus was above our income level, let alone frozen. A (second-hand) home fridge was a luxury preserved for my forties and a freezer even later. And so it was for a large proportion of the population. There was little prepackaging of food and any labels seldom revealed ingredients. Nor was hygiene a priority. Butter was sliced off huge lumps, patted into shape and wrapped in grease-proof paper. Biscuits were sold loose (even Ryvita – a special treat), taken out of big square tins with glass fronts, and popped into brown paper bags. "Biscuit barrels" which adorned many a sideboard made useful containers (and popular wedding gifts) though because they were scarcely airtight the biscuits soon went soft. Commodities such as rice and lentils, packed by the assistants into sturdy blue paper bags, needed careful examination before cooking to extract grit. Vegetables were sold unwashed, which at least meant that city children knew that potatoes and other root vegetables were dug out of the earth, whereas today they might easily think, in the absence of any instruction, that like apples they grow on trees. Natural fruit juice was seldom sold by any other than high-class shops and was very expensive. Lemonade, unless homemade, was merely a fizzy drink devoid of lemon. Vegetarian food was seen as faddy, and only obtainable at "health" shops. Animal rather than vegetable fat was most commonly used by manufacturers, though whatever they used was seldom made known to the consumer, and cakes could be of poor quality, looking much better than they tasted.

A remarkable change has taken place in the food provided at parties and the teas at both secular and church meetings. The "tea-meetings" now known by our community as "fraternals" then only enjoyed sandwiches, cakes, and tea to drink. I have no recollection of salads on the tables, and I don't think they were. My regular task together with Sunday School friend, Beryl Miller, was to turn cheap 1 ply coloured serviettes into "water lilies" – and when lined up on the plates set out on laundered white tablecloths, very grand they looked. After tea a collection "to defray expenses" was always taken, and it is only in comparatively recent years that ecclesias have become sufficiently affluent to offer free hospitality. But while there was little choice of food, there seemed to be no choice at all of whether or not we attended such pleasurable occasions. To stay away was unthinkable. As often as possible we would go to the tea-meetings arranged by other London ecclesias on Saturday afternoons, helped by Dadda's privilege tickets (issued to rail workers and their families at a third of the normal rate together with three free passes per year). A thin penny bar of Nestle's milk chocolate from a machine on the station, beautifully encased in silver paper and a red wrapping, added to my delight, and if I were thoughtful enough it also added to the ball of silver paper which we were rolling up at school to help a needy cause.

One of the biggest changes which has taken place during my life-time is the introduction of pre-prepared foods, instant coffee and tea-bags. Whatever would Grannie have thought of ready-washed lettuce – and of much else familiar to us today? Errand boys on bikes delivered even small orders (presumably if the purchasers could afford to pay for the service) to customers' doors. There were no car boots to fill and no supermarkets supplying fillings. The now ubiquitous plastic bags used by all and sundry were not yet provided. And even after they were, to arrive at a service for worship, or for any respectable occasion, carrying one containing whatever, would have been altogether unseemly.

Understanding food values was given little thought by the average person. It was a case of eating what could be afforded or whatever could be grown. Wholemeal bread was just as cranky as vegetarianism. But homemade loaves, cakes and pastry made with wholemeal flour became our household rule (though Grannie and Grandad didn't conform). "Allinson" bread and corresponding makes, though now in every supermarket and corner shop, were then hard to find. We knew nothing of ready-cut, wrapped bread. The Co-op sold bags of "Allinson", which in common with other flour was contained in cotton bags – with a variety of uses. While Mum boiled them until all the colour was removed, and made large draw-string tea bags for the urn at the tea-meetings, some, poorer than ourselves, sewed them together and made them into pillow cases and (horribly thin?) towels.

Dr Allinson had begun to write just before the turn of the century and had emphasised the need not only for wholemeal products, but also "greenstuff" and fruit, and he stressed the healing powers of nature. I think Dad had become aware of the theory after hearing a lecture given by the doctor. The book he published became our health guide, and because it had no index and because of Dad's esteem for it, he rose to what was for him the laborious effort of making one in a notebook. Natural healing was a useful philosophy if only because we had no money for doctors' fees (though Dad as a worker had become eligible by recent government ruling to be listed as a doctor's free "panel patient"). Herbal tea was brewed from the stinging nettles Dad gathered – to "purify our blood". The drying of elder flowers and peppermint was industriously pursued, and the dried products would later be infused to see us through our various ailments. Today, healthy eating has gained in popularity, and despite the phenomenal advances in medical science (some of which "nature" enthusiasts ignore at their peril), patients are now often advised to let nature take its course rather than resort to drugs with their side effects. The phrase "alternative" medicine was not yet coined but at home that was the remedy. We were seldom ahead of our time but health-wise, mostly we were.

## "Do it yourself"

That the majority of employable women now work outside the home (more today than ever before) has affected not only baking but also sewing. Though the artistic still employ their skills in a variety of areas, and some still excel at home cooking, most every-day clothing, formerly run up on the Singer sewing machine, has been replaced by mass-produced, ready-to wear, off-the-peg outfits. Mending (particularly darning socks) was an ongoing evening occupation for Mamma. Clothes had to last as long as possible, and Dadda's best suit was still good after twenty years. We were far too respectable to patronise grotty second-hand dealers – and today's charity shops had not yet opened their doors.

As a large proportion of the working-class (and the largest part of the population were just that) lived in rooms, the great boom in gardening still lay in the future. And apart from the wealthy with staff, those who did cultivate their little home or allotment patches relied on penny packets of seeds. There was none of the "instant" variety of bushes and flowering plants sold by today's garden centres. Nor were there any D.I.Y. stores. We relied mostly on Samuel's, the local hardware shop, not only for our paraffin oil, candles and matches (and fly papers) but also for hammer and nails as well as the household paint which was so difficult to apply without it going patchy. Utilitarian dark brown was the popular shade. But usually it was the landlord who would be expected to decorate his property, which meant that shabbiness was the condition of most houses, often accompanied by damp patches. A few laminated surfaces and plastic utensils would have been welcome but they were a long way off, even further off than home ownership for "the man in the street".

Ruth's Parents
Jack Ward & May Sparkhall, Wedding Photograph, 1913

# VII
# LUXURY,
# HIGH DAYS AND HOLIDAYS

When my parents were married in 1913, my father's annual paid holiday was all of two and a half days, though I only remember the era when he was given the luxury of a whole week. Even so, by comparison with others, the railway was a good employer. When I was two, only one and a half million manual workers had any agreed paid holidays. Even when I was seventeen less than a third of the total population had a vacation of a week or more. Those who did, had to save up over the year for bus (or the more comfortable charabanc) fares and for the cost of staying at inspection-free "no star" boarding houses, governed by no fire regulations, but splendidly situated at one of the nearer seaside resorts. Holiday makers would quite often buy their own food and the landlady would cook it. It was not until I was eighteen that the 1938 Holidays and Pay Act allowed local trade boards to fix one week's paid holiday for workers.

Bank holidays were not public holidays. But in the absence of our working fathers, Mamma and Auntie Daisy would take me, John, cousin Eunice and her two brothers for a special outing to the London Zoo on Easter Mondays. Clissold Park, with its lake and paddle boats, was another inviting venue, with our climbing up on to the top of open trams on our journeying to and fro. The wooden slatted seats were reversible according to which way we were travelling, and if it rained we could pull up the attached mackintosh "lap tops" which would keep the lower halves of us dry and add to the fun.

As a family we felt specially grateful that we were able to go to the seaside for Dad's one week's paid holiday, thanks to the old – at least he *seemed* old – George Alcock, a stalwart of the meeting. In his early days that worthy gentleman had lived in the Norfolk village of Heacham. He left school when he was seven. His father was thrown out of work, with the result that he, with wife and family (including their little George), had been waved off by the villagers as they made their way in a cart to the workhouse. Though I am not able to comment on their experiences at that particular institution, normally men, women and children were housed separately in such "refuges", usually in horrible conditions, only being allowed visits to each other occasionally. The workhouses were the very last resort for the desperate poor, and the intention of the authorities was to ensure misery and hard labour so as to discourage any from "choosing" to depend on public funds. Gradual improvements were made as the years went on but I recall in my childhood gazing at the mysterious and huge local institution in London (in Highgate?) which was still in use.

George Alcock's parents managed to get established independently again later. By the time of my infancy, and after their deaths, the little cottage (with no modern conveniences) which they had acquired was let out cheaply, together with a beach hut, to families in the meeting who otherwise would have found it more or less impossible to afford holidays. Brother Alcock always had a special regard for those in need. Unusually for a Christadelphian he was an active participant in the Labour Movement, in particular in connection with the Co-op and the railway trade union. He believed that helping to improve the conditions of the poor and those who were virtually slave labourers was a Christian duty. He was outspoken and effective in that sphere as well as at the meeting. He became sufficiently well-esteemed in the railway union to be asked to write its history by which time he had acquired the skill to produce the well-written and authoritative *Fifty Years of Railway Trade Unionism*, published by the Co-operative Printing Society in 1922. It was he who not only made an annual holiday possible for our family but a large part of his library would, after my marriage, occupy pride of place on our home shelves. While I was in my infancy and playing on "his" beach, he was busy accumulating, and getting bound, the monthly issues of *The Christadelphian* which he circulated round the more intellectual members of the meeting (with the written request on at least one occasion "please keep clean")!

Each year we repaired to Heacham using Dad's privilege railway tickets, suitably, we assumed, "third class". By 1956 the lower strata of society, which included the manual workers, had acquired more self-esteem. Third class rail travel was abolished and we only had the choice of first or second class. In the absence of today's car boot our holiday trunk had to be packed (much to my excitement), transported by van to the local railway station, and sent on "in advance". Soon after, we would board the train with its endearing steam, sulphur, sparks and smuts, which after the guard's cheery whistle and flag-waving, chugged its way past the ugly sooted houses lining the track, leaving London far behind, our safe passage relying on the men (earlier including George Alcock) operating the levers up in the signal boxes. Obliging platform staff would hand in at the windows of the small compartments cups of tea at tuppence a time, and, sometimes, on country stations, flower girls would sell to passengers bunches of exotic sweet peas.

If, as I was told, Grannie and Grandad thought they were "in heaven" (metaphorically speaking, of course) when they first received their old age pension (thanks to Lloyd George's efforts), then it was difficult for me to believe that reigning in the kingdom could be any better than at Heacham. After breakfast we tramped our way up the long beach road to "Hawksley", the beach hut. There we spent the day dabbling in the sea or cockling, rambling along the coast, lounging in the deck chairs, "dining" and having tea from the luxuries produced on the "Primus" stove. No perfume (even of flowers!) ever smelt sweeter than the methylated spirits which brought it to life. And when the rest of the family were otherwise occupied John could cycle around on his hired bike and I could wander safely and "lonely as a cloud" on the sparsely populated beach with my imaginary class of schoolgirls. Perhaps it is only in my idealising imagination that I was never bored? But I think not.

Ruth, Jack, John, May Ward at Beach Hut "Hawksley", Heacham
"It was difficult for me to believe that reigning in the kingdom could be any better than at Heacham."

Ruth with parents, May & Jack Ward,
on beach at Heacham, 1926

After so exciting a day what could have been more blissful than the tramp back again to Caley Cottage, there to sink my skinny frame into the depths of the feather mattress, there to breathe in old-time mustiness mingled with the scent of the briar rose, lavender, and box hedging, and be lulled to sleep by the gentle murmur of my parents' voices as they relaxed (for once) in the room beneath, in the glow of the paraffin oil lamp?

The Sunday of that week was the only one in the year when none of us could go uphill and down again to the meeting. There were only "strangers" living in or near Heacham, and to attend any of its churches was out of the question. It was odd indeed that in such a wonderful village nobody was a real Christian but it was just another of those things. We did, however, sometimes attend the local fair during the week, as it seemed more reasonable, I suppose, to play among "strangers" than to pray among them.

May Ward
at window,
Caley Cottage,
Heacham
1920s

Ruth on return visit
1990s

# Some Direct Ancestors

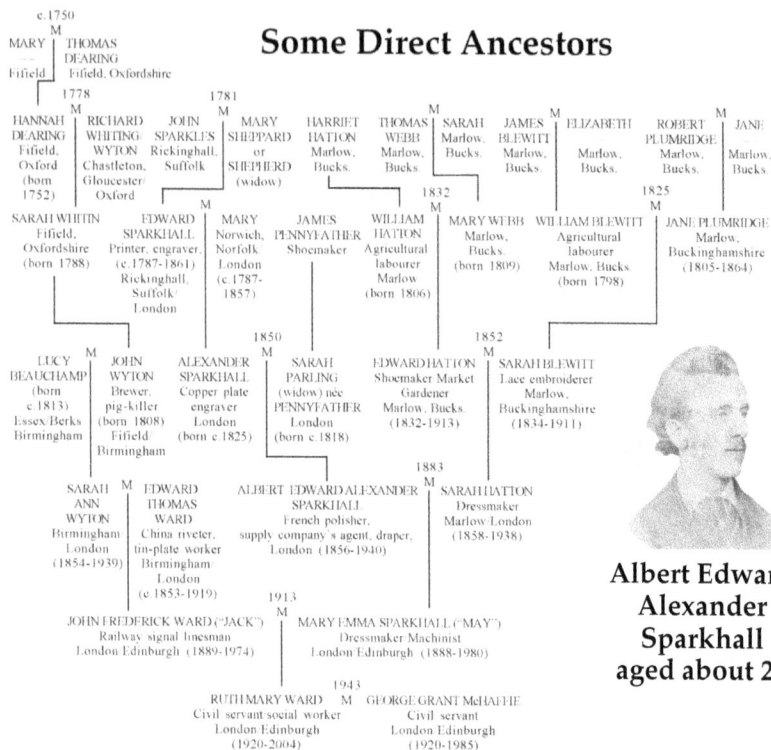

c.1750
M
MARY | THOMAS
--- | DEARING
Fifield | Fifield, Oxfordshire

1778
M
HANNAH | RICHARD | JOHN | MARY | HARRIET | THOMAS | SARAH | JAMES | ELIZABETH | ROBERT | JANE
DEARING | WHITING | SPARKLES | SHEPPARD | HATTON | WEBB | Marlow, | BLEWITT | | PLUMRIDGE |
Fifield, | Rickinghall, | Rickinghall, | or | Marlow, | Marlow, | Bucks. | Marlow, | Marlow, | Marlow, | Marlow.
Oxford | Chastleton, | Suffolk | SHEPHERD | Bucks. | Bucks. | | Bucks. | Bucks. | Bucks. | Bucks.
(born | Gloucester/ | | (widow) | | | | | | |
1752) | Oxford | | | | | 1832 | | 1825 | |

1781
M

SARAH WHITIN | EDWARD | MARY | JAMES | WILLIAM | MARY WEBB | WILLIAM BLEWITT | JANE PLUMRIDGE
Fifield, | SPARKHALL | Norwich, | PENNYFATHER | HATTON | Marlow, | Agricultural | Marlow,
Oxfordshire | Printer, engraver, | Norfolk | London | Shoemaker | Agricultural | Bucks. | labourer | Buckinghamshire
(born 1788) | (c.1787-1861) | (c.1787- | | labourer | (born 1809) | Marlow, Bucks. | (1805-1864)
| Rickinghall, | 1857) | | Marlow | | (born 1798) |
| Suffolk/ | | | (born 1806) | | |
| London | | | | | |

1850
M
LUCY | JOHN | ALEXANDER | SARAH | EDWARD HATTON | SARAH BLEWITT
BEAUCHAMP | WYTON | SPARKHALL | PARLING | Shoemaker Market | Lace embroiderer
(born | Brewer, | Copper plate | (widow) née | Gardener | Marlow,
c.1813) | pig-killer | engraver | PENNYFATHER | Marlow, Bucks. | Buckinghamshire
Essex/Berks | (born 1808) | London | London | (1832-1913) | (1834-1911)
Birmingham | Fifield | (born c.1825) | (born c.1818) | |
| Birmingham | | | |

1852
M

1883
M
SARAH | EDWARD | ALBERT EDWARD ALEXANDER | SARAH HATTON
ANN | THOMAS | SPARKHALL | Dressmaker
WYTON | WARD | French polisher, | Marlow/London
Birmingham | China riveter, | supply company's agent, draper, | (1858-1938)
London | tin-plate worker | London (1856-1940) |
(1854-1939) | Birmingham/ | |
| London | |
| (c.1853-1919) | 1913 |
| | M |

JOHN FREDERICK WARD ("JACK") | MARY EMMA SPARKHALL ("MAY")
Railway signal linesman | Dressmaker Machinist
London/Edinburgh (1889-1974) | London/Edinburgh (1888-1980)

1943
M
RUTH MARY WARD | GEORGE GRANT McHAFFIE
Civil servant/social worker | Civil servant
London/Edinburgh | London/Edinburgh
(1920-2004) | (1920-1985)

Albert Edward
Alexander
Sparkhall
aged about 26

Ruth's great-grandparents, Edward Hatton and Sarah Blewitt
Edward is outside their house at 5 West Street, Great Marlow.

54

# VIII
# MEDICAL MATTERS

Despite the habit of smoking being generally deplored in the Brotherhood, Dr Thomas had thought it permissible for medicinal reasons. In earlier days it had commonly been believed to prevent disease, and in the 18th century it was compulsory for the boys at Eton to smoke a pipe each morning. Although, as explained above, during my childhood there were few warnings of the health hazards, and though "passive smoking" was unheard of, by the time I was six, a member of the medical profession was deploring in the press the danger of nicotine poisoning, referring specifically to the habit being newly acquired by women. The danger emphasised was not lung cancer but mostly the ill-effect smoke had on eyesight. However, Grandad was firmly of the opinion that smoking was necessary and healthy, and would kill off the germs (the predecessors of "bugs"). He must, I'm sure, have destroyed a tremendous hoard and done more than his bit for the health of the capital. Obviously he had not accepted the advice given earlier in *The Christadelphian* during 1882 (before white clay pipes had mostly been replaced by the brown wooden variety).[5]

HOW TO THINK AND ACT ABOUT SMOKING.

This Indian weed, now withered quite,
Though green at noon, cut down at night,
Shows thy decay;
All flesh is hay:
   Thus think, but never smoke tobacco.

---

[5] *The Christadelphian*, May 1882, p. 216

The pipe, so lily-white and weak,
Does thus thy mortal state bespeak;
Thou art e'en such, –
Gone with a touch:
Thus think, but never smoke tobacco.

These were the first two of five stanzas published with the editor's comment,

Transmitted by a correspondent, and acceptable. Ingeniously-constructed, amusing, and wholesome. If it hurt men otherwise exemplary, we give a groan and pass on, with desire for the day that will cleanse and harmonise the whole house of God.

Even as early as the 1860s some Brethren had deplored smoking, and had been moved to write in verse. A nine stanza composition was produced by an Edinburgh member and "respectfully dedicated to those worthy sons of smoke", who were "named and shamed". It commenced with the lines,

My pipe, my pipe, my old companion dear,
    How many a sweet remembrance clings about thee!
Few friends have known attachment more sincere;
    For many a day I could not live without thee:
Now we must part. [6]

Whatever the (as yet unrecognised) danger of passive smoking, I loved playing in the 'grandparental' sitting room with Grandad's home-made paper spills perched in a holder on the mantelpiece ready to light his pipe from the fire, and where the tobacco smoke would curl merrily upward. Grannie would write her now non-existent poems. From time to time I would enjoy a supply of superb Persian kittens produced by Midge (and, of course, by Timmy – though I was uninformed of so insignificant and indelicate a detail).

---

[6] William Norrie, *The Early History of The Gospel of the Kingdom of God*, Vol. II, p. 356

"The tobacco smoke would curl merrily upward."

Mamma was in constant fear lest I should share the fate of the vanquished germs. But, fortified by Grandad's paregoric sweets, I, together with my fluffy playmates, stood up well to the atmospheric conditions, as we savoured the wafting fragrance of simmering fish heads which Grannie was preparing for the feline tea.

Grandad's fumigation was, of course, only a small part of the pollution which filled our lungs, pouring as it did from London's factory and home chimneys. In winter-time we had our "pea-soupers", with the murky fog preventing us from seeing much further ahead than an arm's length and even blackening the sky. I recall scurrying home from school when it was pitch dark at mid-day, wondering with joy (and yet with fear) whether "the End", so often spoken about at the meeting, was about to come. For just as Luke had said in the Bible, the sun was indeed darkened – and who knew whether or not the moon that night would give her light?

The happiness of my childhood and the expectation of joyful eternity was marred by one awful fear. Scarlet fever and diphtheria were common diseases and sometimes fatal. Any child succumbing to either of them was wrapped in a red blanket and whisked off in an ambulance to the isolation hospital. For six weeks there was no visiting, except for parents seeing their children through glass partitions. Being away from home for so long was an experience which I considered would be unbearable. If I saw an ambulance outside a house I would hastily cross the road in case any germ floated in my direction. Had I contracted either of those diseases possibly I would have pined away – but, alternatively, I might have learned to stand on my own feet and gained more confidence. Although I was unaware of it, in fact tuberculosis was a much greater and more prevalent danger, and in the absence of antibiotics there was no effective treatment. However, my fear of any infection was somewhat alleviated because from an early age I was confident that God would hear the nightly prayer Mamma taught me, asking Him to "keep us safe this night secure from all our fears". Inconsistent, of course, but inconsistency seems to be have been one of my perennial weaknesses in a number of ways.

# IX
# THE SUNDAY SCENE

By the 1920s it was not unusual for Christadelphian ecclesias to be owner-occupiers of their meeting rooms, though many still met in hired halls or rooms. Jesus with his disciples had partaken of the Last Supper in a "prepared" upper room. So a room "prepared" for the memorial service, without any ecclesiastical ornamentation was considered suitable for his followers, and preferable, by far, to the edifices of Christendom.

Though the insignia of the Oddfellows or some other worldly organisation decorating a meeting room might be a little distracting, they were considered less inappropriate than Christian symbols, especially the Cross, which had been rendered altogether undesirable owing to its use by "the apostasy", the Roman Catholics, in particular. It was a little strange, perhaps, that Dr Thomas had incorporated in his special picture (referred to earlier) an illustration of the Cross together with the "churchy" IHS, a monogram often taken – incorrectly – to be the first three Greek capital letters in the name of JESUS. But, anyway, when the Saviour returned and was reigning from Jerusalem then the saints (the Christadelphians and any others who had been baptised into exactly the same beliefs), together with the worthies of the Old and New Testaments, would possibly be able to take over the church buildings, and use them in the service of their King. And because of the nearness of that event some considered it inappropriate for any in the Brotherhood to buy either ecclesial or private property

The meeting places were not always as salubrious as they might have been, which was not particularly conducive to worship. Finsbury Park ecclesia met in an upper room at Wortley Hall in the busy Seven Sisters Road. Some of the older members probably found the stairs difficult but, by comparison with some halls, it was large and reasonably commodious. And because, in common with the rest of the population, the elderly received little health care, few lived to become old by today's standards. So the stairs were less of a problem than they would be now. The hall was used during the week by the world, and a fusty odour, a mixture, I suppose, of stale tobacco and alcohol, lingered after Saturday night functions, and greeted us each Sunday.

The morning services were organised in much the same way as today. By the 1920s it seems that any ecclesia which had previously had the benefit of three "exhortations" (sermons) had reduced them to two, while at Finsbury Park there was only one. As a Sunday School scholar, I witnessed only part of the service because we retired at the end of the first hymn from our two rows which were set well back from the body of the hall, returning in time for the teachers to share in, and for us to observe, the weekly breaking of bread (communion). We surveyed the bread and wine with awe (though occasionally pausing to play naughts and crosses), and our return at that particular juncture in the service prevented my wondering as did one small boy in later times, whatever was the secret, mysterious use of the objects hidden beneath the snow-white tablecloth on the (then green baize-covered) platform table.

Our classes for members' children were held in a back room, and there were some fifteen scholars. One Brother objected, maybe not unreasonably, to his delicate daughter joining us since he considered the room too near the lavatories and therefore unhygienic. But the rest of us, probably made of tougher material, managed to survive with no ill effects. My brother John joined the older class on one side of a screen and I the younger on the other. Our teachers, lovingly remembered, were conscientious and dedicated, and respectfully addressed as Mr, Mrs or Miss. If for no other reason, lack of facilities and space prevented us from undertaking any of today's more sophisticated enterprises – but, for me, wearing my home-made Sunday-best, complete with a pretty hat, being told a story by either of the two kind ladies who in turn took our class, and being given a tiny printed text, decorated with flowers, seemed an altogether happy way of spending an hour, knowing that one or both of my parents was/were close at hand. Any possible (but unlikely) boredom was offset by the occasional U.F.O. of the benign variety which came over the top of the screen. But those unexpected interruptions notwithstanding, I think we all, on both sides of the dividing line, were generously awarded two out of two for attendance and good conduct, and for having learned our weekly texts. And at the end of the year we received prizes for our efforts, deservedly or otherwise, I suspect.

In Robert Roberts' day the books given as prizes apparently received even more careful selection than in my own infancy. As he explained in *The Christadelphian*,

> As the question has been asked what sort of books are used for prizes, we may state that the instructions to the bookseller were to send (for selection) a stock of instructive books of a non-theological character. The bookseller, knowing Christadelphian scruples, sent a variety of books tolerably free of orthodox taint, consisting of general story, narrative, useful information, natural history, &c. Literature, in all its branches, however, is too thoroughly steeped in the wine of the harlot to allow of the possibility of getting even books of that description entirely free; so to protect the children from any mischief, the caution "Beware of orthodoxy" is inscribed on the blank leaf of each prize book. The significance of this the children apprehend. [7]

Maybe it was unwise but I never received any books so inscribed; perhaps by my time books had become less corrupted by "churchiness" because less religious material was being published. The "True Zoo Stories" presented to me, for instance, dedicated by its authoress to the "kind hearted little girl who gave her mother's umbrella to the monkeys and watched them tear it up", did suggest mischief but couldn't be described as being "steeped in the wine of the harlot".

---

[7] *The Christadelphian*, August 1869, p. 244

61

The annual Sunday School examination was approached with trepidation. It was so important, I knew, to do well. Every year there were not only weeks of "recapitulation" on Sundays in accordance with the syllabus but for me there was, as well, careful coaching by my mother. Not surprisingly, in view of the intensive tuition, I gained high marks – and gained yet another prize as did all candidates whose parents were keen members of the meeting.

On special Sunday afternoons the prize-givings took place and sometimes the meeting's visiting speaker for the day was invited to present them. The scholars would perform a well-rehearsed "demonstration", creating, for example, a lighthouse, each with our building "block" and reciting our "piece" impeccably mastered "off by heart". Finally, the electric light at the top would shine forth. As many of us had as yet no electricity at home this climax added something remarkable, especially as Dr Thomas considered electricity to be a manifestation of the Holy Spirit. And since it was the Lord who made "all things bright" our pioneer must have been right. Moreover, Robert Roberts, after observing the difference between the new electric lighting in Edinburgh's Princes Street and "the dingy, dull, yellow flicker of coal gas jets", had written in *The Christadelphian* during 1881, "There can be no doubt that electric light (*alias* spirit light) will be largely employed in the age to come...".[8] But neither of our pioneers would have been impressed that Britain's first public building to be illuminated by electricity was the Savoy Theatre in London in that very year. In 1890 it was recorded in *The Christadelphian* that a hotel in Samaden was using electricity for cooking when it was not required for lighting. And it was commented that this indicated that when God makes his "feast of fat things" in Jerusalem it "will not be accompanied by the discomfort and uncleanliness inseparable from the use of coal and other fuels".[9]

We produced one demonstration which encouraged us all to count our blessings. That was the first occasion when I was allocated the solo singing of the verses in my squeaky voice, with the other children joining in the chorus. Readers will not be surprised to learn that it was not only the first time that I had such honour bestowed upon me – but also the last. And looking back I realise now that in our audience were many sad hearts who would have been glad that, as children, we thought it so easy to count our blessings and had no understanding of the sorrows which life could bring.

Visiting speakers from other meetings were always made exceedingly welcome by the meeting, and "entertaining" them for dinner and tea was a privilege. They usually had to rely on public transport like most people, and every effort was made to supply their material needs in the best possible way between the morning and evening services. Sometimes their hostess (never their host) for the day would leave the meeting during the last hymn so that she could catch an earlier bus or

---

[8] *The Christadelphian*, December 1881, p. 559
[9] *The Christadelphian*, January 1890, p. 24

train, get home and put on the cooker or at least the kettle, though such premature departures drew criticism. But those were the days before automatic ovens and microwaves, when to get to and from the meetings in the absence of a car, and to have the traditional Sunday roast at the ready when the speaker (and sometimes his wife) arrived home with his hosts was no easy achievement.

Owing to my father's frequent Sunday work and probably because we were not among the intelligentsia of the ecclesia, we never entertained the visiting speaker. But although our Sunday fare at home would not, I suppose, have been up to "speaker" standard, Mamma, with the help of the kitchen range, managed to produce every week a hot dinner at high speed (and butter beans remain in my memory as an enjoyable Sunday speciality).

She always made it clear to me that much though she admired the Brethren who officiated at the Sunday services, Dadda was in no way inferior to them. She was right, of course, for it was better to eat our dinner in the kitchen at the old table with our own uncomplaining Mr Smiley, than in a select dining room with a "speaker" whose smiles were left at the meeting room. But though it was impressed upon me that being a platform Brother was no guarantee of Christian love round the domestic hearth, I found that hard to believe in view of my high regard for them.

In the winter, our kitchen usually doubled up as the sitting room, with or without the washing above our heads on the pulleys, but on Sunday afternoons a glowing fire in our upstairs "front room" warmed our toes if not our backs. On the grate was fixed a decorative iron trivet for boiling the kettle, and the fire was excellent for making toast for tea which was often spread with dripping (solidified fat from roasted meat). I could set myself up in a corner or under the table with its heavy, fringed cloth, either of which provided accommodation every bit as enjoyable as the "Wendy House" which later came on the market, now superseded by the even more luxurious accommodation enjoyed by today's children. If Dadda were not at work he would play his few self-taught hymns on our peddle organ, and we were frequently reminded (I think because the tune was an easy arrangement) that "Life is the time to serve the Lord", and because of his love of cultivating the soil we perennially 'ploughed the fields and scattered...'. Meantime we were ever hopeful that the "call-out man" would not knock on our door, which would mean that Dadda would have to change into his old clothes, get on his bike, go to whatever mishap had occurred "down the line" and, of course, miss the evening lecture. But it seemed even worse (at least to me) when he was called out on Christmas Day.

Sometimes on Sunday afternoons I would peer between the long, heavy cotton lace curtains and see the Salvation Army coming up the road. And when they gathered together in their smart uniforms, the brass band struck up stirring tunes and the ladies in their bonnets sang so lustily and shook their tambourines, I loved it. Although Grandad had ignored the instruction in *The Christadelphian* when it disapproved of smoking tobacco he endorsed the editor's views on the Salvationists. The Army was, the editor had commented,

> doing good gutter work; cleansing the moral sewers a little; taming and training a certain part of the savage population of Tarshish [referred to in the Bible and believed to be Britain], in preparation, possibly, for the use that we know the Lord intends to make of that country in the glorious revolution that is approaching.[10]

Soon after that authoritative pronouncement was made in the magazine, a baby boy was born who, though he would never become a savage "gutter" child, was one of the disadvantaged with an over-burdened (but deeply caring) mother struggling to feed too big a family. How old he was when he first came in contact with the Salvation Army I don't know. I think it was some time after an artist engaged him as a model for her painting, arranged with his mother for him to stay off school for a day, and presented him with the largesse of sixpence together with a parcel from the kitchen.

It is doubtful if he, who would grow up to become my Dadda, ever availed himself of the farthing (or was it the

---

[10] *The Christadelphian*, February 1890, p. 62

ha'penny?) breakfasts which the Salvationists supplied to deprived children. Even so, he was delighted with the farthing's worth of cake crumbs which he gleefully bought from the baker who fired the cakes of the local housewives since they had no ovens. And it was the Salvation Army whose kindness and faith held out to him a welcoming hand and perhaps even 'trained' the fresh-complexioned, curly-headed youth. But in any event it was he who, when a little older and very "respectable", and after finding the job of delivering buttons to a dress-making firm, fell in love with Grandad's eldest daughter, my "Mamma-to-be". Doubtless she would have been warned by Grandad, as I would later be warned by him, that she should not be courting an "alien". My particular "alien" (not yet part of the scenery, of course, any more than I was) had been a lifelong Sunday School scholar and was soon to be baptised but "alien" in Grandad's eyes just the same.

Anyway, his eldest daughter dutifully "sewed" the Christadelphian seed, as well as the firm's dresses. She drew the Salvationist away from the Army, introduced him to "the Truth" and subsequently responded to his "Daisy, Daisy, give me your answer do..." (which long after her acceptance he would still be whistling). That song came from the popular music halls – which on principle Dad would not have frequented even if his purse would have stretched to buying a ticket. But he would have heard it in the streets and round about, and, as the Salvation Army said, 'Why should the devil have all the best tunes?'

Not surprisingly my parents were ever grateful to those worthy people, and remembered their tolerance of the drunkards Dadda had watched hurling abuse or even dangerous missiles on their would-be rescuers, or pouring the drink, which they could ill afford to buy, down their shining brass trumpets. He would sometimes sing to me one of their songs which was a reminder that each of the depraved was born an infant, and (hopefully) "Some mother rocked him in his cradle to sleep". So when a gentle lady in uniform, who, despite any ridicule, was not deterred from standing up and singing up for Jesus, came knocking on the door after a Sunday afternoon performance, I was sent to give her a few "coppers" for the needy. "But," warned my mother, "don't tell Grandad". And I never did.

Despite Robert Roberts' view of the Salvation Army, apparently there was no objection to a brass band being used as a preaching aid, even though the players were "aliens". At a special effort in Northfield, Birmingham, in 1899 "Mr Cadbury's brass band" was allowed to lead the way, it being agreed that the music to be played would be "in harmony with the Truth".

When the shadows of evening fell on Sunday afternoons and just before the heavy brown wooden Venetian blinds were lowered, I could watch for the approaching lamplighter with his long pole, and see him making his way up the road stopping at each lamp-post to set the gas mantle glowing. He was a reassuring figure and when he (or just possibly his relief) would return at the break of day to reverse the procedure, he seemed to be the only person in the world awake beside myself. Little did he know how often I, a poor sleeper, listened for his welcome footsteps at the crack of dawn. Again, unknown to him, he carried not only his pole but also a lesson, for we so often fail to realise how much our daily round and common task, reliably performed, can mean to an unseen observer.

As well as the Sunday School examination in the summer, there was the eagerly awaited "treat". Spending a whole day in the fields or at the seaside was an occasion not to be missed, for there were few such opportunities. As compared with today's Sunday School trips the "treats" were inexpensive and more prim and proper, with girls dressed like miniatures of their mothers except in skirt length, and boys dressed like miniatures of their fathers except in trouser length. And the home-packed food was, as usual, very plain.

We ran our races in Hadley Woods and though not quite in keeping with the words of the apostle Paul, we all received prizes. Sometimes we went to Alexandra Palace and paddle-boated on the lake. Best of all we boarded a steam train to Southend. There we dabbled our feet in the sea and could buy a penny "Snofrute" or a tuppenny ice cream "brick" from the Wall's "Stop me and buy one" man, who, tricycling up and down the promenade with his ice-box, was enjoying the sea air possibly as a change from his winter-time occupation of Wall's sausage production.

# X
# "TREATS"

The select "morning" Sunday School combined at the "treat" with the much larger and more boisterous "afternoon" school. On Sundays the latter was attended by a large group of children from the Campbell Road vicinity, one of London's notoriously deprived areas where crime flourished, but where we hopefully distributed the *Glad Tidings* magazine. For many of those children the happy occasions would be their only holiday (unless they managed to enrol on the register of some other dedicated but "alien" Sunday School and so became eligible for their "treat" too).

By the 1920s the attitude of many in the Christadelphian community toward the deprived and disadvantaged in the world was changing from that commonly held in the body's infancy. In earlier days many were themselves living in extreme poverty; so much so that, for example, some in Birmingham were unable to attend tea-meetings because they couldn't afford to contribute for the food. Robert Roberts sensibly had abolished the collections, and the expenses were covered by the Sunday morning "free-will offerings". Understandably, the poorer members who comprised a large part of the meeting had little to spare for doing "good unto all men". Moreover a strong feeling was held, and is still held by some, that hardship suffered by "outsiders" was punishment from God, and therefore the community should make no organised attempt to relieve it (Jews excepted). It was felt that energy should be concentrated not on the alleviation of social ills, but on preaching true doctrine in contrast to the falsehoods of "priestcraft". Thereby we could destroy the hope that any "social gospel" could bring the kingdom of God to fruition.

Gradually, however, when many among us were becoming more affluent, there crept in the idea that preaching "the Truth" might be done more effectively if we offered a cup of water to the thirsty rather than confining our resources to drowning erroneous beliefs. To what extent our community should support "outside do-gooding" would by the 1960s become a subject of heated argument but I need only comment here that during my infancy, Finsbury Park ecclesia was among those who tried to bring "a knowledge of the truth", together with material help, to those unfortunates who previously had been seen by Dr Thomas as "the swinish multitude" to whom "the kingdom's gospel was not proclaimed".[11]

At Christmas-time there was the annual Sunday School party, and as at the summer "treat" there were assembled the two groups of children, with a recognisable but unmentionable social gap between them. Altogether about a hundred children were at the party. I recall Mamma's (discreet) concern after I had persuaded one of the tiny "afternooners" to sit on my lap (that is, on my new party frock – which she had so carefully created). But perhaps, just for once, I was trying to put into practice one of those familiar texts, "Little children, love one another". Anyway, nothing was "picked up" and no damp patch soiled the frock, so all was well. And whether we looked pretty or tatty, whether our odour was sweet or sour, we "classlessly" joined in playing the well-worn games, "Gathering nuts 'n May", deciding whether to be an orange or a lemon, and proclaiming "Heigh Ho, here we go – the farmer wants a wife". On one occasion an enterprising young Brother clad entirely in rubber tyring circulated among us. He made an excellent advert for the Michelin firm (I think it was) whose pneumatic tyres were replacing the old hard variety on carts and motor vehicles. Advert, or not, we were delighted by the novelty. The delectable white sandwiches together with the iced cakes (supplied by our baker Brother Miller, my parents' favourite speaker and friend Beryl's father), were regaled with enthusiasm, more eagerly by some than by others, for the tea provided an opportunity for the hungry to be sent away full of good things.

---

[11] *Herald of the Kingdom and Age to Come*, – a periodical John Thomas published in America – April 1852, Vol II, No. 4, p. 109

Afterward we settled down to the customary "do-it-yourself" entertainment, recited our recitations and sang our songs. Performance was not compulsory but nearly so, for we felt under an obligation to please everyone, and the morning scholars knew that a higher standard was expected of them than of the "afternoon" contingent. We were at liberty to offer light contributions, and "the man in the moon" who came down too soon was altogether acceptable. That there might ever be a man in the moon never entered our heads, and any such concept would have been unacceptable to our elders for it would have been seen as contradicting the Psalmist who proclaimed that "The heaven, even the heavens are the Lord's: but the earth hath he given to the children of men" (Psalm 115:16). The then editor of *The Christadelphian*, Brother C.C. Walker wrote in 1926, "We have sometimes speculated as to whether the moon may not be, as it were, the hotel of the angels...". [12] That was, I think, a very nice idea but one which today, it seems, we have to dismiss.

On occasion there would be a cantata sung by the seniors, though I must confess that none of the uplifting wording of their choral effort has stayed with me. But I do remember the less classical contribution rendered by two excellent songsters and which pleased my musical taste enormously, "There's a hole in my bucket dear Liza, dear Liza...". The human memory is strangely selective.

On at least one occasion Mamma took me along to the enjoyable party of the nearby Camden Town meeting. That ecclesia, if I remember rightly, and I think I do, belonged to the Advocate section of the community composed of those members who had refused to accept the amendment made to Section 24 in the Statement of Faith on the matter of responsibility to judgment. (The "Unamendeds" are still prominent in North America.) After 1898 they were rejected from fellowship by Temperance Hall, and were therefore in much the same position as the Suffolk Street members who had been withdrawn from in 1885. There was considerable goodwill between the two groups and it was not long before Camden Town joined Finsbury Park ecclesia, bringing with

---

[12] *The Christadelphian*, January 1926, p. 13

them Brother Will Douglas who would become my Auntie Doris' husband.

## A Special "Treat"

Together with a few other "bona fide inside" children, I was taken along when a Christadelphian group visited the British Museum. The official guide, apparently unimpressed by our well-scrubbed, snowy-white socked and demure appearances, didn't believe that we children could be trusted to keep silence during the tour. He did not, of course, know how well practised we were at sitting silently on hard chairs with legs dangling for the duration of long lectures. However, we managed to gain his reluctant acceptance and to the delight of the Brother who nobly negotiated on our behalf (and to the equal delight of our proud parents) we were later commended for our good behaviour. That gentlemanly guide would have raised no objection to our presence, of course, had he been aware of our genuine eagerness to view his exhibits which we were convinced would prove the truth of the Bible stories in which we were so well-versed.

In more recent years, as a dignified senior citizen, I spent a fascinating morning in the British Library, then housed in the Museum. At lunch-time I set out through the elegant galleries in search of lunch. In the "good old days" complaints had been made that the smell of boiled cabbage from the refreshment room pervaded exhibition areas (which scarcely created a suitable environment for the exploits of the kings of Nineveh). But, by now, this problem had long departed. Instead, there was an excellent non-cabbage boiling restaurant, supplying delicacies of wide variety, and if any odour escaped then it was the delicious fragrance of coffee.

Remembering from childhood the revered nature of the establishment, the good behaviour expected and the excellency of the long-ago guided tour, I tripped decorously through the (by then chatter-filled) halls and was almost knocked off my feet by an enormous schoolbag being whizzed circular-wise by some irreverent end-of-20th century monster.

The British Museum has been a continual source of interest for Christadelphians as well as for innumerable "outsiders". When I was twelve, thirty large cases containing material written in cuneiform were brought from Ur of the Chaldees by Sir Leonard Woolley, the celebrated archaeologist, all helping to strengthen the faith of Bible lovers and to add interest to Museum exhibits. In 1844 a German scholar had found the Codex Sinaiticus in St Catherine's monastery on Mount Sinai. In 1859 it had been transferred to the Tsar of Russia (the "king of the north" expected by Christadelphians to be the invader of Israel at the "Last Day"). There could scarcely have been a more unsuitable location for so important a manuscript. In Britain an appeal fund was set up for its purchase from the Soviet government when it was offered to the British Museum for £100,000. The government paid £1 for every £1 donated. King George V generously gave £100 and his wife, Queen Mary, gave £25. The Christadelphians sent "a modest contribution". I was fourteen in the very month that the Codex was secured for the nation – a celebratory birthday indeed![13]

## Yet Another Treat

The "Dorcas" played an important role in my childhood. The afternoon sewing class had been introduced in 1913 just after my parents were married, and its purpose was to make clothes for the many needy in our community. Mamma was greatly honoured to be made secretary and to "go into print" announcing its existence in *The Fraternal Visitor*.[14] The class was, she told me later, the highlight of her week. With all the experience she had gained in her daily dress-making before marriage (as well as her making clothes for her younger sisters) she was a valuable asset.

Because she was the only member with a young child, I was allowed to accompany her not only to the class but also to the ladylike, behatted and delightful annual outings to Kew Gardens where I could dance beneath the cherry trees laden with their pink and white blossoms, secure in the love of my elderly friends. I knew, of course, that in winter-time the boughs would have shed their blossoms and leaves, and "Kew" would lie beneath the snow. And I gradually came to realise that those sweet Sisters would become "the leaves around us falling" as would so many others dear to me.

AN OFFER OF CLOTHING.

Dear Bro. Barker,—The Sisters of the Finsbury Park Ecclesia, London, having started a sewing class, would be glad if you will kindly insert a notice in the *Fraternal Visitor* to the effect that in the event of any ecclesia having a case needing clothing, and supplying particulars, we shall be pleased to assist them to the best of our ability. Communications to be sent to address given.—Yours fraternally, (Mrs.) M. Ward (Secretary), 67 Westfield Road, Hornsey, London, N.

Just occasionally the Dorcas Class would be invited home for afternoon tea. We couldn't get out the silver because we hadn't any, and we couldn't hang out any flags because my

---

[13] *The Christadelphian*, February 1934, pp. 77-78
[14] *The Fraternal Visitor*, November 1913, p. 335.

74

one little Union Jack would not have made a good enough display, but we did our best with the precious patterned tea service kept only for such grand occasions. Dainty sandwiches spread with Burgess's (always Burgess's) sardine and tomato paste and Mamma's home-made bread made high-quality fare for the Sisters. At least, we thought so!

## Dorcas Class Outing

The Dorcas class outing to Kew Gardens, c. 1930

**Back Row** *(left to right)*: **Sisters Pescod, Rowley, Lowe, West, Moore, Lavy, Jackson.**
**Front** *(left to right)*: **Sis Owler (a great-aunt of Janice McHaffie, née Adams, and a superb catering organiser), Sis. Streeton, May Ward, Ruth Ward, Doris Sparkhall.**

75

# Sunday School Outing

Finsbury Park Sunday School Outing to Chingford, 1913
May Ward and her younger sister Doris at front
(left hand side)

### Report in the Fraternal Visitor

LONDON *Finsbury Park.* — Our Sunday School excursion took place on July 30th, when the scholars and a number of brethren and sisters journeyed to Chingford. A most enjoyable day was spent by all, which was in no small measure contributed to by the beautiful weather, for it was a most glorious day of brilliant sunshine, tempered by refreshing breezes. ... W. W. ROWLEY, Secretary. (Ecclesial Notes, *The Fraternal Visitor*,[15] September 1913, page 281)

---

[15] *The Fraternal Visitor* was the magazine published by "our" side which had been expelled from fellowship in the major division of 1885. The other side was called Temperance Hall.

# XI
# "PROPAGATING THE TRUTH"

As often as possible and while I was still quite young we returned on Sundays to the public evening lectures, after our tramping uphill and down again. I was sent into the last sweet shop before we reached the meeting to buy some scented floral (or blackcurrant) gums to stave off any boredom I might suffer. I was never allowed to buy sweets from any poor fellow, most likely a disabled ex-serviceman, who would have a tray hung round his neck holding his goodies, and who would stand outside the park gates, trying to earn a living. He kept his stock under his bed, I was told, which seemed to me such a horrible thing to do, and not at all in keeping with our respectability.

The Brethren and Sisters at the meeting listened intently to the lecturer, looking up the many texts quoted from their treasured black (always black) Bibles. The genial faces of those earnest, dark-suited Brethren remain clearly etched in my memory though I fear I did not concentrate with the intensity of my elders. Sometimes, as an alternative entertainment, and together with the floral gums, I occupied myself with such irrelevant occupations as categorising into their several colours the hats which decorated the Sisters and added colour to the dull surroundings. There was one old Brother who, to my surprise, also sat in the meeting wearing a hat, but it was explained to me that it was to keep his head warm, and in the circumstances I suppose the apostle Paul would have overlooked his apparently unseemly behaviour. But, anyway, his "ridiculous headpiece" (using Robert Robert's vocabulary) was of a nondescript shade, so fell outside my statistical analysis.

Despite my respect for all the proceedings, nevertheless, when the hand on the clock had gone past eight, I hoped the speaker would soon sit down. And I knew that once he reached the (seemingly weekly) point of explaining the importance of adults being immersed then the end was nigh. An invitation to return next week (which we would gladly accept), a final hymn and a prayer (hopefully not too long), gave the signal that I could scramble off my chair and go to see Mr Edgar who would give me yet another sweet and make me laugh (and probably helped more than was realised toward my becoming a Christadelphian).

But I did learn, too. We were all to take the Bible (which was so "plain") just as it stood, though when Jesus spoke about "everlasting fire, prepared for the devil and his angels" he didn't really mean that there was a devil and accompanying wicked angels, nor that there would be an everlasting fire. Obviously I didn't understand all that was said, especially when the erudite lecturer explained the meaning of words like "ruach" in Hebrew and "pneuma" in Greek but I knew that whatever he said, he was right. Indeed, so appreciative was I of the Brethren's words, that in my early teens and during the school holidays, I, with Indian ink and mapping pen in hand, produced a condensed version of the vital aspects of their preaching and "published" a mini "hard-back", entitled "Christ, the Messiah".

In the same year, 1935, the first Penguin paperback was published and that has had the privilege of gathering fame as a collector's item, whereas my production has merely gathered dust. However, though not in any way due to its lack of merit (of course), but merely to the perennial dearth of "interested strangers", and, apart from the dust, it is still as "good as new" nearly seventy years later – even if the "gold" lettering on the cover has become, like its author, decidedly faded.

Although, for many people, trust in God had been shattered by the horrors of the 1914-1918 War, yet in the early years which followed some turned to Him for comfort. Christadelphian lectures were frequently based on the "state of the dead", which possibly accounts for my early understanding that "no heaven going" was *the* first principle.

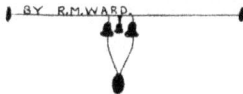

CHRIST, THE MESSIAH.

CHAPTER I   HIS HUMBLE BIRTH.

"Jesus, meek and gentle,
Son of God most High
Pitying loving Saviour,
Hear thy children's cry"

"For unto us a child is born, unto us
a son is given, and the government shall
be upon His shoulder, and His name
shall be called Wonderful, Counsellor, the
Mighty God, the Everlasting Father, the
Prince of peace." Such was the prophecy
proclaimed by Isaiah in his day of the
Great Messiah who was to be our Saviour.
That Saviour was not born in a palace
however, but was found by shepherds
lying in a manger. So Christ was born in
a stable, and was laid on straw in a manger, but it was He who was to be the one to
suffer the agony of the cross and to drink
that dreadful cup of pain that we poor
sinners might be saved through His grace.
This was He, the only begotten Son of God,
although born of humble birth in a humble
place yet He aroused the jealousy of
King Herod who tried to take the life of the

1

## "A condensed version of the vital aspects of their preaching"

It was a subject which attracted public interest more than most. That was not surprising since one in twelve of Britain's population had been killed in the recent conflict when women had lost not only husbands, lovers and brothers, but also one, two and even three of their sons, many fighting for a cause they did not understand.

Spiritualism flourished in the post-war years. As John Burnside wrote in *The Scotsman* in April 2001, "...after the Great War, Europe was a continent in mourning, wandering from one seance room to another, hoping to catch a glimpse, a smile, or a word of forgiveness from the recently departed". Those who came to hear our message at the meetings were given no comfort. The lecturing Brother made it clear that however virtuous and dedicated to his church and to God was the departed loved one, unless baptised into "the Truth" as taught by Christadelphians, then he or she had no pre-eminence above a beast, and there would be no more remembrance of him or her under the sun. The dead would merely fly forgotten as a dream dies at the opening day.

Our members would have assured any strangers present that "we are so pleased to have you with us" but grieving souls must have gone away in deeper depression than they came, for the message they received spelt out in no uncertain terms 'abandon all hope ye that enter herein'. The lecturer would, by way of exception, have made it clear that for those living, there was still the opportunity to gain eternal life. But our community, largely untouched by the horrors and the carnage of war, and the Brethren on the platform, mostly unseared by the fearful pain of bereavement, would, for the most part, have given little thought to the devastating effect their preaching would have held for mourners who, without their loved ones, found little interest in their own survival. But however unpalatable, "the Truth" had to be preached.

"Strangers" would have realised that Christadelphians were not suffering from war-weariness, for Dr Thomas had left the community in no doubt that Armageddon was to be eagerly awaited and it would usher in a "belligerent state of things" which would continue for forty years (though by 1939 a footnote in *Elpis Israel* indicated that it would not necessarily extend for that time).[16] Lectures on prophecy and especially on developments in Palestine were also frequently delivered. One visitor who recorded his observations on a Christadelphian lecture when I was seven commented, "It lasted for an hour, and was concerned as much with politics as with religion". Addresses dealing with the destiny of the British Empire were distinctly political, for the Empire was seen as exceedingly important in relation to God's plan, and attracted politically-minded outsiders. Sometimes, unimpressed by our message, they declared their opinion in no uncertain terms. On one occasion a few years later, teenage brother John, squeaky clean and all dressed up in his Sunday best, with "Brylcream" keeping every hair in place, offered a visitor a leaflet as she left the hall. But the large lady swept on her way with the Parthian shaft, "Out of my way, you well-fed gutter snipe". But if my mother's pride in John was a little

---

[16] John Thomas, *Elpis Israel* (1939 edit.), p. 449

ruffled we were not unduly perturbed by such incidents for, proudly, we saw ourselves as "Few in number little flock, by the world despised, forgot".

In 1917, three years before I was born, Turkish rule in Palestine had been overthrown, and General Allenby had triumphantly entered Jerusalem. The way was now open for Britain to encourage the establishment of a national home for the Jews. My infant years saw the lecturing Brethren drawing up charts and from them indicating the exciting political developments, explaining how near we were to the Second Coming of Christ. In earlier days visual aids such as "dissolving views" (lantern slide pictures enlarged as light passed through them on to a screen) had been considered suitable for use at Sunday School parties to introduce aspects of the Truth to the children. But by some they were frowned upon as a way of preaching during lectures. However, by the early 1920s the community had updated itself a little, some earlier views had "dissolved", and magic lantern slides showing developments in Palestine shone forth, brightening Sunday evenings especially for the rising generation. Even "movie picture" shows were given at special efforts. In 1926 a film called "The Land of Promise" was shown at the Broadway Bioscope Cinema and was attended by six hundred seated viewers with others standing, and our very own Recording Brother Frank Tanner ("Secretary" as our ecclesia preferred to call him) with his "stentorian voice" chaired the occasion. Wilfred, his youngest son, was in the same Sunday School class as myself, so that gave me reflected glory.

In a personal capacity many were eager to spread the good news. One brother carried one or two Jaffa oranges in his pocket "when they were on sale in the fruiterers' shops" (i.e., "in season"), together with a copy of *Glad Tidings* containing news about the colonisation in the Holy Land. This was thought to be convincing material to show to any interested stranger.[17]

---

[17] *The Fraternal Visitor*, January 1928, pp. 6-8

—Canadian Magazine Post.  One Copy Post-free for One Year, 1/6.

# OCTOBER 1915.

# GLAD TIDINGS

## OF THE COMING-AGE

THE HOLY CITY

"How beautiful are the feet of them that preach the Gospel of Peace, and bring Glad Tidings of Good Things."—*Romans* x. 15.

Edited by WILLIAM GRANT.

## CONTENTS

# PRICE ONE PENNY

All Business Communications to be sent to the Publisher,
**WM. M. SMITH,**
13 Annandale Street, EDINBURGH.

All Letters to the Editor should be addressed to
**13 South Gillsland Road,**
EDINBURGH.

"THY KINGDOM COME, THY WILL BE DONE ON EARTH."

"THEY THAT ARE ACCOUNTED WORTHY TO ATTAIN TO THAT WORLD (AGE) CANNOT DIE ANY MORE."

*GLAD TIDINGS, Cover, October 1915*

82

# XII

# MISERY OF
# "THE HUNGRY THIRTIES"

The General Strike, when workers supported the protest against the reduction of the already appallingly low wages and the terrible working conditions of miners, came and went without achieving success or bringing any alleviation of their misery. The mine owners won and the starving men could do nothing but give in and return to work

Before the strike began, in February 1926 it was reported in *The Christadelphian*, quoting from the *Daily Mail*, that

> "Last summer the extremist leaders of the miners made no secret of their intentions. They proclaimed them beforehand from every housetop. They arranged a great system of conspiracy, which they called the 'triple alliance,' to paralyse every industry in the country and to hold the nation up to ransom."[18]

In fact, the leaders of the miners were trying to improve the lot of those they represented, but their efforts brought scant sympathy from the well-heeled. The occasion provided an opportunity for university undergraduates to 'do their bit' in maintaining the enjoyable *status quo* in which they had been reared. They cheerfully drove the buses and became conductors, complete with their trilby hats, plus fours and college scarves. They, together with many other volunteers including schoolchildren, operated the various services and thereby minimised the inconvenience caused to the public, most of whom were more concerned with getting from A to B, as well as receiving their coal deliveries, than they were over the plight of the exploited miners and their families. In that

---

[18] *The Christadelphian*, February 1926, p. 74

period of our history women who could drive were from the upper classes. Significantly, forty per cent of the volunteer drivers during the strike were women – the well-fed bored with time on their hands. For them the strike was so jolly.

I was told at home that we were very fortunate because Dadda didn't go on strike (presumably because Christadelphians thought striking inadmissible). So at least the weekly wage was not withheld from our household. I do remember, however, my mother telling me that 'unions were good things' and in view of the conditions of the working classes at the beginning of the century (and even more so in earlier times), undoubtedly she was right. Today, workers are enjoying the benefits which unions have struggled to negotiate over the years, with vast improvements in conditions. Many Christadelphians are now members of them even if they do not approve of all the actions taken, and those who do not belong are not averse, it seems, to enjoying the benefits won.

# XIII
# SIGNS OF THE TIMES

It was during the year of the Strike that I, aged six and apparently a late developer, first noted the importance of the "signs of the times". I remember Dadda sitting in the kitchen reading his newspaper. *The Daily Herald* had originally been a weekly paper but after the Great War had become a daily. It was published by the Labour Party (formed in 1900) and was popular with the working classes. Dadda commented on the unrest in China, and I gathered it was a notable portent of the return of Jesus. Gradually I came to understand the enormity of the war which was expected to break out. That my gentle father would gather up his weapons and join happily in wading in the blood of the wicked was either not told me or the information did not penetrate.

My reading skills at that time were only at "the cat sat on the mat" level. But after moving on and improving my literary ability, I was able to observe that Dadda's interpretation of events in his own little way was in keeping with that of the erudite Brethren. The editor, Charles Walker, had commented in *The Christadelphian,*

> No doubt China will "wake up" to the conditions of Western militarism, and the 400,000 yellow men will provide a new and terrible contribution to "the war of the great day of God Almighty".[19]

Dad enjoyed his *Herald*. And I, too. But my interest was confined to the exploits of "Bobby Bear" whose illustrated adventures were recounted in the paper's daily strip. That was the era (possibly only as remembered?) when temperatures in summer and winter were as expected. But torrential rain from time to time seems to have been a constant feature of Britain's climate. Dadda, who had to work in all

---

[19] *The Christadelphian*, January 1927, p. 34

weathers, would cheerfully quote Bobby as and when appropriate, "What dreadful weather we are having. Quantities of rain!". But as my awareness of the importance of political developments grew, so I realised that my father's real interest was not in Bobby Bear but in the Russian Bear, believed to be the "king of the north". And in 1927 that king was expected to make his massive offensive against Palestine – with the arrival of Armageddon and the conquering Jesus Christ.

Meanwhile, people in the world were occupied with other thoughts. Since the end of the Great War women over thirty who were householders or wives of householders (many of whom who had played a big part in ensuring victory by their work on munitions and taking over jobs which previously had been for men only) had been allowed to vote in the country's General Elections. This had not been seen as a pleasing development by all, especially by the male population. But at Easter in 1927, Mrs Pankhurst's and the other suffragettes' ambition to obtain the franchise was better realised when every woman over the age of twenty-one was given the vote. This privilege was greeted with abhorrence in some quarters, especially by a certain Colonel Applin who warned, "It must mean taking on grave responsibilities which would perhaps be too grave a burden on women", while *The Daily Mail* warned of the danger which now beset Britain, "The time may come when if women decide to use their power, they will be able to dominate the State". This seemed no unrealistic threat for so many men had been killed during the War, while women, on the whole, had survived. And when the War was over, the latter were not so keen on being just the "little housewives", even less the doormats, as most had been earlier and to which status they were expected to return.

Strangely, it seemed to pass unnoticed by Christadelphians that the new electoral arrangement about to be introduced nationally merely reflected the long-established practice in the ecclesias. Sisters had frequently been numerically predominant, and it was therefore their voting power which had decided which Brethren should be in office and which Brethren (often to their chagrin) should not. But the new nationwide freedom was understood by the community as being in the same category as the trouble in China and therefore a "sign of the times". Prophecy was being fulfilled for it was believed that women gaining power indicated decadence (Isaiah 3:12) and decadence was expected as "the End" approached. In the 19th century Mr Gladstone had thoughtfully excluded all women from the class of those "persons who can travel without check along all the lines of public duty and honour...", and the Brethren were happy to agree with him that the female gender was "stamped with disability for the discharge of executive, administrative, judicial, or other public duty".[20] Any woman who voiced herself in public was considered by John Thomas to have adopted "the brazen attitude of a public oratrix".[21]

In 1928, the year of the first election after women over twenty-one had been given the vote, King George V was gravely ill and not expected to recover. He was deeply revered by the nation and criticisms of the royal family (justifiable or not) were unthinkable. Our community followed the biblical injunction to honour the king and he received praise as one who revered the Word of God. The Christadelphians were pleased that our "Royal family daily read the Bible, and must be more or less familiar with the divine decrees...". It had been hoped (as it had been hoped for his grandmother Queen Victoria and his father King Edward VII) that King George would be the monarch to hand the British crown to Jesus at his Second Coming,[22] after Britain and her colonies had assisted in the 'war of the great God Almighty'. If, however, King George died before Jesus came, then since he had not been a baptised member of the Christadelphian community

---

[20] *The Christadelphian,* July 1892, p. 267
[21] *Elpis Israel,* 1849, p. 109
[22] *The Christadelphian,* January 1929, pp. 34-35
Photograph of King George V from Roger Vaughan Photograph Collection. Reproduced by permission.

but had been the Defender of the corrupt Faith of the Church of England, he would inevitably be annihilated.

But I had no need to bother myself with such complexities and could leave it to the wisdom of the Brethren while I continued to occupy myself with the less disturbing perplexities of Bobby Bear or of Tiger Tim in my newly acquired *Rainbow Annual*. In any case, King George recovered from his illness and went on to reign for another eight years.

# XIV
# WE ARE 'NOT AMUSED'

After the First World War "picture houses" were popular with the lower classes. *The Fraternal Visitor* quoted the "Cinema" that

> ... over 20,000,000 people, mostly of the industrial classes ... sit in semi-darkness and silence for several hours each week with their eyes and thoughts fixed on our screen. The industrial classes do not listen to sermons nowadays, nor do they read the newspaper leaders.

The cinema, its advocates urged, was "the great educational agency of the age".[23]

In 1928, during the same year as the crisis caused by his Majesty's indisposition, the local "pictures" were advertising the latest advance in technology. After the War, when Britain, France and Germany were financially exhausted, the production of films had passed largely to America. By 1927 wireless sets were detracting from the number of Americans who had been paying to see the "movies", but the industry was revolutionised with the introduction of the phenomenal "talkies". When I was eight they were being shown locally, with huge adverts attracting our attention. Earlier productions had flickered and the noise of the projectors had been disguised as far as possible by pianists who played melodies to match the mood on the screen. With the arrival of sound films and the building of grand, carpeted cinemas resembling palaces (but, I understand, with no lavatories), together with the introduction of colour, the audiences changed in character. They improved in class and the "pictures" gradually lost their reputation of being flea pits. And unfortunately for the pianists their services were no longer required.

---

[23] *The Fraternal Visitor*, July 1919, p. 162

But flea pits or not they were no more officially permissible for Christadelphians than was voting in the country's elections. How many kept strictly to the rule I am unable say, but quite a few did not. Rightly or wrongly my parents made the very occasional afternoon visit and I was taken along to see the latest wonder. I remember being impressed by the sweet little Shirley Temple, as I thought her to be. But nobody need have feared for my spiritual welfare for, in general, I thought the Hippodrome quite horrible – with its ornate plushiness, the darkness, the uniformed usherette guiding us to our seats with torch in hand, the peculiar scent mixed with tobacco smoke, while appallingly dolled-up actresses and smarmy actors crossed the screen with cigarettes hanging from their lips. Many children "of the world" flocked to Saturday morning cheap matinée performances, sometimes gaining admission by taking jam jars as their entrance fees. Inevitably, the silver screen influenced every-day life. Whether we attended the pictures or not, we all came to know about Walt Disney's Mickey Mouse, who appeared in New York in 1928. Apparently it was originally planned that he would feature in a silent cartoon, but the production was overtaken by the advanced technology and his debut marked the first fully synchronised sound cartoon. Thereafter he became common parlance.

"OK" and many other American expressions were gradually adopted by the British, even by John, though I thought they were not used by "nice" people, and I did so want to be "nice". But now, more than sixty years later, I discover that the internationally known lexicographer and dictionary editor, David Guralnik, who died recently, considered that "OK" "best expressed the creativity of English-speaking Americans". It was originally an abbreviation for the deliberately misspelled "oll korrect", and its first known use was in a 19th century dictionary. "Nice" I might have been – but characteristically behind the times!

I can only suppose that it was because of my especially unsophisticated life-style that the pictures didn't attract me. On the rare occasions when I saw a film it was a relief to emerge into the daylight and the fresh air, and to escape from the worldliness which I had been taught was so despicable. I much preferred my homely occupations, making a dolls' teaset from the garden clay, or communicating with the fairies in the blue, always blue, lupins. (The multi-coloured Russell variety was not introduced until I was seventeen.)

Upbringing had ensured that I was a "Mamma's (and Dadda's) girl". That particular breed was less thin on the ground then than it is today so I never lacked friends of a similar ilk. But while some of my peers would eulogise on film stars and I became familiar with their names, I kept my adoration for my teachers or the dear chatty people at the meeting, for dear to me indeed they were. And their chatter provided much more interest than any cinema "talkies".

By the 1930s "going to a dance" was popular among young "outsiders". Many of the dancers met their "young men" and "young ladies" in the ballrooms. Whatever new steps were being introduced in America were soon adopted in Britain. But Christadelphians did not "go dancing" (even less than picture-going), and the very thought of doing so when we reached teenage years would never have occurred to those staunchly in "the Truth" or those considering accepting it. The fear of worldliness has always been a problem for puritanical communities, not the least for Christadelphians. Each new development has been greeted with dismay and disapproval by the elders. But I and my "meeting" peers (those brought up "properly") simply accepted that where the world went, we did *not* go.

## "Listening In"

Since my early infancy the "wireless" had been making its way into neighbours' homes, often initially as a home-made crystal set with ear phones attached. "Listening in" at home, even though it reaped disapproval from the Brethren, was not regarded as sinking to quite so low a level as joining in with the activities of worldly companions. My first recollection of the innovation is the wire trailing round a chair – in itself a novelty since in the absence of electricity we had hitherto been wireless in the true sense of the word. We had to tread softly for if the connection was in the least disturbed, so would be the reception which, if I remember rightly, was never clear at the best of times (though I have since discovered that it could be really good). It all seemed marvellous indeed, even more so than the gramophones with their big black trumpets which neighbours with money and time to spare had planted in their parlours and "front rooms" in place of their aspidistras, and which enabled their frivolous owners to dance the tango or the foxtrot under their own roofs. We, of course, preferred our cheap and cheerful aspidistra which seemed to have the capacity to stay alive in whatever environment, and, wonderfully, if I held up to my ear the big shell stationed by Grannie's specimen, I could even hear the music of the far-away roaring sea – so much sweeter than worldly dance tunes.

It was when I had reached the age of two that the "British Broadcasting Company" had begun regular broadcasts. Members were soon reminded that Jesus would not have listened to the wireless and neither should they. However, our body never went so far as some sects who totally rejected the newly arrived foe. One community who, peculiarly, thought that they alone were the elect of God, decreed that any of their brethren who acquired a wireless were to be excluded from eldership. We can be sure that objections in whatever religious group were made largely by active members, busy in the swim of life. They couldn't imagine the company that music or even the sound of a human voice trying to predict the weather, could bring to the lonely disabled and elderly housebound.

Not only the small sects but also the mainstream churches were not all that welcoming to the new entertainment. Their leaders were not convinced of the desirability of broadcasting religious programmes, and saw the wireless as a threat – despite Director John Reith's stringent standards and his dedication to the Christian cause. Listening to religious deliberations on earphones was thought irreverent. When in 1923 permission was sought to relay the Armistice Day service and also a royal wedding from Westminster Abbey, the church authorities refused permission. They considered that "the services would be received by a considerable number of persons in an irreverent manner, and might even be heard by persons in public houses with their hats on".[24]

Dearie me! – hats on or off seem to have created a perennial headache for those aspiring to be Christians. Anyway, Christadelphians remained level-headed and no total ban was imposed on the wireless, though opinions remained mixed. It's just a pity that at the age of five I was unable to read and appreciate the charming little poem which appeared in *The Fraternal Visitor*, entitled "Listening In", and which used the latest craze to spiritual advantage. There were nine stanzas. The first and third read,

> Listening in; are you listening in,
> When does the Broadcasting really begin?
> God in His Heaven is speaking, I know.
> What is the message He's broadcasting now?

> Crystal Receivers, your head should instal
> Aerials of Hope, you can tune to the call;
> Shut out the noise of earth's traffic and din,
> God's speaking from Heaven, are you listening in?[25]

Before long it was realised by an increasing number of members that the wireless could be an asset, and even those who had regarded it with initial disapproval or suspicion began to appreciate its potential. John Reith (later Lord Reith), who directed it until 1938, was a rigorous Scottish Presbyterian. Prospective employees were asked if they believed in Jesus Christ. In the early years the programmes were mostly music. News bulletins did not begin until the evening so as to prevent competition with newspapers. On Sundays only the weather was broadcast before noon and so avoided any rivalry with the churches. Of course, Christadelphians would never have allowed the apparatus to affect their attendance at the meetings, but then they did not belong to "the churches".

I don't remember when we first acquired a (second-hand) wooden fretwork-fronted "loud speaker" containing its fragile silvery valves, and the messy, "acidy" accumulator which had

---

[24] Bradley, *Marching to the Promised Land*, pp. 190-191
[25] *The Fraternal Visitor*, December 1925, p. 325

to be taken from time to time to a shop for recharging. We, at home, never had one of the grand cabinet sets which were gradually emerging from the manufacturers, and which some of the more skilled with time to spare were industriously making – with Honduras mahogany recommended by the household encyclopaedia, though deal would do for the back. Apparently no thought was given to the depletion of the rainforests, nor to the flooding which eventually would wreak havoc on the dwellings and lives of the indigenous poor.

In any case, the diminishing of the forests would have seemed immaterial to Christadelphians, for much the same reason that some members today are unconcerned about environmental pollution. The kingdom was imminent and the year 1927 was noted as marking the end of the 1290 period in Daniel, chapter 12. The New Year was greeted by our members with another of those engaging poems, which, apparently with poetic licence, overlooked the long and dreadful war expected at Christ's coming, and the years of hostilities which would subdue the nations. It was headed "1927" and the first four lines ran,

"The time is at hand!" Do you think of it still,
As a great time of blessing, of peace, and goodwill?
Does it outweigh the pleasures of present-day gain,
With its promise of life in a world freed from pain?[26]

Many thought that between 1927 and 1932 it was "certain" that the Master would return, though Robert Roberts had more cautiously thought 1933 a more likely date. But, in any case, after Armageddon there would be no need to cut down forests for the weapons of the vanquished armies would provide enough fuel for seven years (Ezekiel 39:9,10). Today it is rather harder to imagine surplus wood remaining after hostilities, even if nuclear missiles or other weapons of mass destruction were not employed.

When I was ten in 1930, the Luxembourg "station" began broadcasting light entertainment programmes, which attracted many listeners. Soap manufacturers financed the early "soaps", all of which brought more frowns from critics. I

[26] *The Fraternal Visitor*, January 1927, p. 3

recall very little listening-in at home and can only remember becoming "glued to the set" during the annual Oxford and Cambridge boat race (first instituted in 1850) which always attracted enthusiasm at school, at least in London, when every child who could find a penny or so wore their "favours". Oxford with its dark blue was chosen almost exclusively by boys, and Cambridge with its pale blue almost exclusively by girls. A tiny celluloid doll clad in a pale blue-feathered skirt was my treasure indeed.

John Reith soon discovered the problem of pleasing or displeasing audiences, both those who supported the churches and those who didn't. However, even in the early days, some in our body saw the wireless as an opportunity not to be overlooked. In 1928 a Brother in Wales informed the editor of *The Christadelphian*, that he had written to the BBC offering an address by a member. A polite letter declined acceptance though in Australia and Canada our community had been able to broadcast and had received many interested enquiries. But our editor did not "feel enthusiastic over the matter ... we are not ambitious of being mixed up with 'trumpets of uncertain sound'", and he awaited the time when "The Lord shall roar out of Zion...". Nevertheless, he included a letter in the magazine written to the *Daily Express* by an "outsider" who would have liked the BBC to open its programmes to "disputatious arguments". But he himself thought such arguments ill-advised – and admittedly if the pattern followed were to have developed into anything like the vitriolic arguments which had raged between our pioneers and those who disagreed with them, then his judgment was remarkably wise.

Although never included in our hymn book, in 1928 "The First Radio Hymn" written by a Congregationalist author was published in *The Christadelphian*.

> Imperfectly we know Thy thought,
>   Yet dare recall Thy ways of yore;
>   Behold, O Lord, what Thou hast wrought,
>   And bless the radio, we implore.[27]

---

[27] *The Christadelphian*, April 1928, p. 180

Only a few years passed before listening-in came to be seen as a blessing by a number in our community and it provided an excellent theme for one of our Sunday School demonstrations. More seriously, in February 1933, the editor of *The Christadelphian* had referred to

> the extraordinarily interesting Imperial broadcasting experiment in which the King spoke from his home literally to "all the world" in the Imperial sense of Luke ii. 1: "There went out a decree from Caesar Augustus that all the world should be taxed." We were mercifully spared any talk about taxing, and the King's message was a simple greeting to the British dominions all round the world. It was most impressive to hear on that cold Christmas afternoon [1932] the voices of Canadians, New Zealanders, Australians, Indians, ships in Egyptian ports, etc., describing their conditions of climate, of night and day and so forth. One passed in a moment of time from the snows of Canada to the heat of the Antipodes. And one realised as never before the possibilities of the literal fulfilment of the prophecy of Rev. i. 17: "Behold he cometh with clouds and every eye shall see him...".[28]

*The Fraternal Visitor* likewise commented on the occasion when the "King Emperor" was able "to speak to his people throughout the mighty British Empire". The words of the Prime Minister were quoted when he referred to "that most wonderful event today, unique in the history of the world, when the King addressed all his people from the rising to the setting sun".[29]

## The Small Screen

An even more impressive move toward the entertainment and education of the nation occurred in the year 1925 (when I

---

[28] *The Christadelphian*, February 1933, p. 81
[29] *The Fraternal Visitor*, January 1933, pp. 1 & 19

first attended school though the two events were unconnected). The Scot John Logie Baird produced the first moving image on his television screen after a fifteen-year-old office boy (afraid of the bright lights) had been bribed with half-a-crown to sit for the experiment in the London attic workshop. "Every eye" as well as every ear was soon to be acquainted with "live" world events, and the entertainment which would be offered would not be as profitable to the mind as Lord Reith and the BBC governors intended.

Developments in television with the first broadcast in 1936 took place in Alexandra Palace, where (unaware of the advancing technology so close at hand) I often played with my cousins in the grounds and meandered through the vast halls. It was good to listen to the organist Goss Custard (yes, that *was* his name) as he practised on the enormous pipe organ, or we amused ourselves popping pennies in the slot machines to see moving pictures of footballers – I remember no others – and not many of my own pennies were so recklessly spent.

With the outbreak of World War II, the development of British television was suspended. The Germans already had sets in their homes which proved valuable in acquainting them with their troops' victorious and phenomenal progress. After the end of hostilities the announcer in England appeared on the screens of the privileged few and commented, "As I was saying before I was so rudely interrupted...". From then on TV would gradually invade almost every home in Britain, and many would be the "rude" (very rude) interruptions. Ian Bradley in his *Marching to the Promised Land* (1992) has reminded us that in Broadcasting House in London, and set above the lifts in the entrance hall, is the inscription which reads,

> This temple of the arts and muses is dedicated to Almighty God by the first Governors of Broadcasting in the year 1931, Sir John Reith being director-general. It is their prayer that good seed sown may bring forth a good harvest, that all things hostile to peace or purity may be banished from this house, and that the people, inclining their ear to whatsoever things are beautiful and honest and of

good report, may tread the path of wisdom and righteousness.[30]

The inscription is in Latin and as few today will be able to interpret it, few will note its irony.

While Lord Reith was the director, the establishment was run "as though it were an extension of the church" (even though the "extension" was not gladly received by those establishments). So far as he was concerned it was "taken for granted that it [the wireless] should be a strongly Christian organization". By the 1950s the lives of the masses were being revolutionised by television, "the idiot box" (as one 1950s school teacher referred to it). Reith had no affection for new development. He believed in the word being spoken without any adornment as it was in his father's pulpit. He would have been appalled had he been able to see a journalist's

Broadcasting House,
built 1932,
Headquarters of the BBC
Photograph: www.Bigstock.com

comments in an article entitled "Entertainment to death in the cultivation of stupidity", published in *The Scotsman* in July 1996. The writer observed that it is "worth asking how a civilisation of so much clever technology comes to be cultivating stupidity for profit". In the same paper and in the previous month, it was commented that a recent survey had indicated that infants between the ages of two and three spent more than eighteen hours a week watching television and only three of those hours were supervised by adults.

---

[30] Bradley, *Marching to the Promised Land*, pp. 189-190

Wise parents are vigilant as to their children's viewing, but undoubtedly it wields enormous influence unknown to earlier generations who lived before the invasion of our sitting rooms by the "black beast", as one Sister called it. Even so, for those who are discriminating, TV offers a window of opportunity for education in its many varieties, and inquiring minds can be helped to keep abreast with world problems and developments. Moreover, as with the wireless, it brings welcome company to the lonely and housebound.

**Remains of Jack and May Ward's 1930s Radio**

("Defiant Model M 234", now much battered after being deposited in a shed, and showing a make-do-and-mend approach where a new inside has been fitted into the original cabinet!)

"Speed thee, brother, on thy way"

# XV
# "HAVE YOUR OWN RAILWAY"

In the mid-19th century the development of the railway had captured people's imagination. Robert Roberts had described the experience of travelling from Birmingham to Edinburgh by rail which took approximately nine hours. "You step", he wrote, "into a comfortable covered box with wheels, take your seat, and wait a certain length of time, and then walk out".

By the turn of the century, private motor cars had made their appearance on Britain's roads, and motoring was growing in popularity among the wealthy. After the 1914-18 War, the expensive, mechanically unreliable monstrosities were often driven by chauffeurs, but the classy young, after returning from the perils of the battlefields, soon took to the wheel. Dare-devils accompanied by their "flapper" girlfriends drove through town and country often oblivious of danger to themselves and even more oblivious of danger to others.

In the 1920s rapid growth in the motor industry was underway. In America Henry Ford mass-produced his cheap models, the "Tin Lizzies", and set a pattern for British companies who followed with Baby Austins and Morris Minors. When I was four the Scottish Motor Show adopted the slogan "Be a motorist and have your own railway", but very few Christadelphians were able to travel on the new 'rails'. They had avoided "the front" during the war and their limited budgets ensured they stayed at "the back" on the arrival of the motor. But in common with much else, only a little further on in history and it was all change.

The motor bike, with or without an attached side-car, was better matched to our community's purses and was acquired by a few of the more go-ahead. Wife and sometimes small children could be packed in and there was no problem in parking immediately outside the meeting rooms – or anywhere else. Once second hand cars became available then more members were able to join the motoring brigade, and some joined it who could ill afford to do so (as I was given to understand at the time). Naturally, our household continued (perforce) to set a good example and we still made our way on Shanks's pony with the occasional help of the buses, especially for our return journey uphill and down again from the meetings. Fortunately on that route only the single-decker buses ran, for the new, covered-in double-deckers alarmed us, our thinking that they looked so top-heavy, and fearing that they might topple over.

The increasing popularity of motoring received a mixed reception. The disquiet was expressed in Parliament that the great British reputation for breeding horses would suffer, and one Member of the House claimed that the traffic put us in more danger on our streets than that faced by workers in the coal mines. Gardeners saw a diminishing of the gold dust dropped by the horses which was eagerly gathered up by the likes of Dad at every opportunity. But the pollution problem which would eventually develop was unforeseen. Motoring was making a hole in the pocket but surely never in the ozone (the "ozone" we then understood to be the health-giving air of the open country or seaside).

The first fatal accident had been suffered by a lady who was on her way to Crystal Palace in Hyde Park in 1896, and the coroner at the inquest had hoped that 'such a thing would never happen again'. No hope could have less realisation – and not surprisingly so, for "untested" motorists (a sixteen-year-old could buy a car licence and a fourteen-year-old a licence for a motor bike) took the law into their own hands. The rule of keeping to four miles an hour with a man in front holding a flag had not endeared itself to a nation becoming increasingly industrialised in the 19th century. And in the 20th, after the imposition of a twenty mile per hour limit, it was invariably ignored, so much so that it was abolished. However, a number of restrictions were gradually introduced, at first only of a primitive character. At intersections the drivers were expected to blow their horns and many pedestrians, though advised to cross the road with care, failed to heed the warning with disastrous results.

Though the ecclesias continued the practice, it became inappropriate for us to sing, "Speed thee, brother, on thy way", but if the Brother in question had any armour he was well advised to cling to it, for the fatalities in 1930 resulting from the comparatively small number of vehicles on the road was double the number of those in 1960. As cars took over the highways and byways, it became essential for everyone's wellbeing that drivers should learn the hitherto unobserved code,

The rule of the road is a paradox quite
When driving your carriage along.
If you keep to the left you're sure to go right.
If you keep to the right you'll go wrong.

The author Noreen Branson tells us that when a Bill on motoring was under discussion in 1930, the MP for Bermondsey claimed that six hundred trees lining the road in his constituency were demolished in a year by cars mounting the pavements. The government had to take further action and this time take it quickly. A thirty mile per hour limit in built up areas was imposed – and was expected to be observed. The manufacturers did their bit by supplying handy appliances such as driving mirrors. The Minister of Transport had declined in 1924 to make these compulsory and is quoted as announcing, "I am not satisfied that the universal adoption of mirrors or reflectors to enable drivers to see overtaking traffic would generally assist in the prevention of accidents, though their use in cases where the driver is unable to hear or see signals from behind is no doubt a convenience for overtaking traffic".

Advice was issued by the ever-encouraging motoring companies on preventative measures to avoid having to empty car radiators on cold nights. Radiator lamps and muffs complete with the newly introduced zips 'to keep Jack Frost at bay' gradually became popular, and an increasing number of drivers found it unnecessary to put their vehicles off the road for winter – though in the absence of heaters, the travellers needed plenty of blankets. We all became accustomed to the growing assortment of aids for motorists and pedestrians alike – the glass orange balls, toning yellow lines stretching round the margin of the bay, pretty coloured lights, cats' eyes, zebra crossings, and obliging green and red male midgets, instructing us when to cross and when not to cross. Back in 1868 when John Thomas was writing *Eureka*, the authorities had seen the need for some traffic control. Photos taken at the time reveal that jams caused by horse-drawn vehicles in central London were not dissimilar from our twenty-first century motorised version. At one intersection in the city, multicoloured gas lamps, changed manually by policemen, were introduced. America had gone ahead (as so often) by introducing electric lights in Detroit in 1920, and when I was six in 1926, Britain's "firsts" were erected in Piccadilly Circus. A "sign of the times" indeed – one which passed my notice. But gradually as my childhood proceeded it became evident that freedom to do as we pleased was not necessarily to our advantage, and jay walking was left to the foolhardy. By the end of the 20th century half a million people would have died on the roads in Britain and 30 million would have been injured.

Go-ahead women of the world were soon trying their hands at the wheel, but as we would expect, the Sisters dutifully hung back, and it was generally accepted that their role was to be driven. "The Motor" for 1924 assessed the position. An article headed "Women and Safety Last" gave statistics to prove that women drivers were the main cause of accidents, an allegation which has since been dismissed. It was claimed, "Vanity, of course, is the chief reason why a woman ever seeks to learn to drive". "Women" it was alleged, "only learned to drive to show off". And as I toddled along in my home-made white corduroy outfit, with my hand grasped firmly by my mother, lest I should stray from the straight and narrow, I could never, even for one moment, have thought of any better reason. Undreamed-of was the free taxi-service which would be provided in the years ahead for frail churchgoers, possibly by more women than men (since it is the "weaker" sex who have a greater inclination toward attending worship).

# XVI
# LEARNING SYMPATHY

By 1928, in the same year as King George's worrying illness, the world was on the brink of economic collapse. In the following year, 1929, the Wall Street stock exchange in America crashed. Share holders were devastated. Few in the community would have understood the nature of the calamity and were not directly affected. Like my parents they knew nothing of shares, apart, of course, from the Co-op and the essential sharing with one another, the family, near and extended, and with their neighbours. But we did become aware of some of the consequences. Britain was hit badly, especially the industrial areas of the Scottish Lowlands, the North East of England and South Wales.

Collections had long been taken to help the unemployed in the Brotherhood but by 1927 more work had become available and less assistance was required. But once again distress signals were sent out as "the Slump" plunged members into the unemployment which continued throughout the "hungry thirties", not only in Britain but throughout the world. The Dorcas classes worked overtime to produce "undies", winceyette nighties and sensible hard-wearing clothing, especially for the children. There was a proportionately high number of Christadelphians in South Wales, and the pathetic distress being endured there became well-known to us all.

Though London was not one of the areas most seriously affected, I gradually became aware of the differences in people's standards of living. On our way to the junior elementary school at St Mary's (which by then had become "mixed"), Joan and I crossed the path of the "rough" children making their way to the "tough" school. Our neatly clad selves, with Joan's long, chestnut (rag-curled) "corkscrews" daintily bobbing up down, might not have been the instigators of the verbal warfare which arose between us and

105

"them". But though I was fast becoming an expert on the fulfilment of the promises to Abraham, my standard of ethics inclined to stay on the level of the law of Moses, and an eye for an eye seemed altogether appropriate. We avoided the physical violence which young males so often enjoy and stuck to the aphorism that "sticks and stones will hurt my bones but words will never hurt me". But "our" mothers were not disposed to having their darlings victimised by hooligans and somehow "their" mother was located in the Campsbourne slum area and was duly contacted by mine. The outcome was not quite as we expected, for we learned of the pitiful struggle Mrs Ascott was having to feed and clothe her family. As so often, and as I would learn so many times in the years that followed, we found that to know all was to forgive all. Thereafter squabbles ceased and our parents did the little they could to help. Living next door to us was Auntie Gladys who needed a charwoman and at that time could afford one (with Uncle Sid being a white collar worker in his "good job"). Mrs Ascott was duly appointed and any spare clothing passed on to her. Enid, my little cousin and regular playmate, had some beautiful clothes which made lovely cast-offs. It was at that point I came to understand that however poorly Dad was paid, yet we had a regular income and that while the Campsbourne children had to make do with whatever they could find (often from those much despised second-hand shops), Mum on her old treadle Singer could "run up" new clothes for me from much-sought-after remnants or from Hawkin's sixpence farthing (or was it three farthings?) per yard "Miss Muffet" cotton prints.

Not many of my classmates were among the most deprived though I do recall one little fellow with lovely dark brown eyes who I realised was a "poor" boy. The girls at school were always addressed by their "Christian" names and the boys (to make them manly, whatever was meant by "manly") were addressed by their surnames. "Easter", as he was called, was always being naughty, and my virtuous self, now apparently sprouting some sort of social conscience (or whatever), graciously bestowed on him one ha'penny a week on condition that he was good. I doubt whether my Lady Bountiful generosity lasted long and I do hope that when it

106

was withdrawn poor Easter managed without it. However, Miss Nash, our young teacher, who was everything she should have been – except that she was not a Christadelphian – was quite capable of keeping her class in order without my help. When I asked if she would make a contribution to my autograph album (a possession we all aspired to have) she duly complied. Instead of writing some silly couplet as most did ("By hook or by crook I'll be last in this book"), she inscribed a quotation from Shakespeare, "To thine own self be true, and it must follow as the day the night thou canst not then be false to any man". One day, she said, I would understand its meaning – and I did, but found it was not at all easy to put into practice, for to determine our motives is not a simple exercise.

**The R101 airship on its first test flight, Westminster, 1929**

The R101 set off for a maiden voyage to India on Saturday 4 October 1930, the first stop intended to be Egypt. Mechanical problems and gusting winds caused an unexpected landing in France and the airship then caught fire. 48 of the 54 people on board died, including Lord Thomson, the Air Minister, government officials and most of the designers. It was the worst airship accident of the 1930s and put an end to British airship development.

(http://en.wikipedia.org/wiki/R101)

# XVII
# THE END OF THE WORLD?

In the Christadelphian community the signs of the times continued to be watched eagerly. When long before (in 1871) the Pope had lost "territory and political power", this had been seen as indicating "the End", and deep disappointment had followed when it proved otherwise. But now in 1929 the Pope was seen rising again in influence and this, too, was incorporated into the prophetical scheme. His gain was thought to be indicative of the great and final climax of history, and eagerly once more the Brethren and Sisters stood on tip-toe. Technological and scientific developments could also be seen as moves toward the climax. On a Saturday evening in October 1930 we rushed out on to the street to look skywards, and saw the R101 Airship passing over. But on the way to the meeting in the morning the newspaper placards were splashed with large letters announcing that it had blown up. Clever though mankind is, there is always a reminder not far away of his frailty and helplessness.

Though the imminence of "the End" has always featured largely in Christadelphian teaching, it has nevertheless been thought appropriate for members and their families to continue in their normal work patterns. So at school we were encouraged to busy ourselves with our early education and at the age of eleven I moved into the "scholarship class", coming under the tutelage of the amiable Mr Stewart who seemed to have outstanding tolerance toward the absurdities of his youthful charges, and was ever ready to mediate between them in their petty quarrels.

There was that dreadful day when Enid Line (despite being one of my "best friends") splashed a large blob of ink from her inkwell (situated a few inches behind my shoulders) and soiled my new lemon frock – "on purpose" too! My complaint seemed so enormously justified and important. But it would have frozen on my lips, and the kindly face of Mr

Stewart – the peacemaker among his silly little girls and boys – would have clouded with grief had we all known that in another ten years Enid, the treasure of her parents, would be wiped out of existence by the explosion of an enemy bomb.

And how many others, I wonder, of those little ones, "regardless of their fate", sitting in their rows of double, iron-framed, oak desks struggling with the multiplication tables, those "Enids" and "Easters" in class after class, in school after school, town after town, nation after nation, would, as they reached the sweet blossoming of their youth, become statistics on the multiple lists of fatalities, blasted to death in enemy territory, shattered in the skies, torpedoed in the seas, or buried beneath the rubble of their own homes. How true it is –

Thine is the burden of the coming years;
    Their weal or woe.
Their joys and griefs, their laughter and their tears,
    We would not know.

# XVIII
# FROM "RESPECTABILITY"
# TO MIDDLE CLASS

Soon it was time for me to sit "the scholarship" taken by eleven year olds to assess whether they were academically suited to move to a Secondary (Grammar) school, where they could receive education up to the age of seventeen or thereabouts. The alternative was the Senior Elementary where they would be trained mostly for artisan and domestic work and would leave school at fourteen.

Secondary education was fee-paying, but up to 119 out of every thousand working class children who passed the "scholarship" were awarded free places by the local authorities. In some areas, at least, there was a little subtle manoeuvring so that most places were given to boys. I recall being warned by my mother that scholarship or not I could only move on to Hornsey High School for Girls if I were offered a free place. However, Dad's income was low enough to ensure that no fees were payable and so I went, and since most of the uniform required was too expensive for us to purchase, Mum once again employed herself on the indispensable "Singer". Owing to the delay in the completion of an additional section to the school-building, the holidays were extended and since newborn cousin, Rosemary, had just arrived in her home round the corner, I, by the stroke of such good fortune, was allowed to stand and stare at the miracle in the cradle: one of life's highlights – enhanced by the scent of Woodward's Gripe Water.

Children often accept whatever comes along, and perhaps it was because I was a first-generation secondary school pupil that my parents were largely unaware of how valuable was the opportunity. I feel I would have appreciated it more had the privilege been stressed. The influx of girls from a local "posh" private school somehow dislocated my earlier zeal for

111

trying to be "at the top", and I fell back into the "could do better" group until near the end of the course. And even then I was motivated by nothing better than having an extraordinary crush on our (quite ordinary) biology mistress, and therefore set out to please her by absorbing knowledge, cleaning the aquaria, her lab bench etc. after school hours, or spending the holidays painting large class-demonstration posters to illustrate a cross-section of the columbine or the metamorphosis of a frog. Well done, Miss Furniss! But looking back I realise how alarming is the influence which role models can play in our lives, for so often young people have the misfortune of choosing the wrong one, and there is little parents can do about it.

Hornsey High numbered about four hundred girls. After being opened as a private exclusive establishment it had been taken over by the local Education Committee. And the hat regulation so often rearing its head in theological circles reared it even there. At all times on our way to and from school we were to be "behatted" with cream panamas in the summer and black velours of the same shape in the winter, both bearing a band with school colours and badge. Lady-like behaviour, especially in the streets, was a high priority, and we were instructed never to give away to the needy any uniform bearing our school badge. Only the art teacher apparently had risen to car ownership. She was very tall, and in her "Baby Austin" made quite a remarkable sight. Otherwise, the mistresses walking to and from school were able to observe our behaviour as we also trod there and back (our lady-likeness continued by our changing into house shoes when we arrived).

There were the occasional serious lapses in behaviour, of course, incurring wrath, reprimand and "conduct marks" but nothing physically "abusive". Just when I was all geared up, with lines learned, to play the part of Shakespeare's Richard II in the class play, there was the disaster of collective punishment, and all plays were cancelled – because some hooligan pupils had thrown toilet rolls round the playground. Sadly, Richard II I was "not to be". It wasn't fair – but then life seldom is. So at least that lesson was learned, and since then I've spent a lot of time trying to explain to myself and to any who ask why it is that so often the innocent suffer and the guilty couldn't care less. I've never arrived at a satisfactory answer, and nor I think has anyone else. That it's "all God's will", as some say, doesn't seem right, for it leaves us with a very odd God – certainly not a caring one. But perhaps those who comment (irreverently) "God knows!" might be more correct than they realise.

Today we are all well aware of the disciplinary problems so many teachers endure. "Not like the good old days", we say. But although I recall no lack of class control in my early years, there was a lamentable lack of it by some of the mistresses at Hornsey High, despite the school's excellent reputation. The smallest teacher I remember, suitably named Miss Littlejohn, commanded total respect and attention, yet the larger variety (one in particular) experienced classroom chaos. When Miss Reid distributed test papers they were promptly returned to her desk, sticky burrs were thrown on her back while she wrote on the blackboard, or we enjoyed the "fun" of disappearing under our desks. Not surprisingly she eventually had a nervous breakdown. And how had I conducted myself? I joined the rest – mob behaviour I suppose. But, on the odd occasion, the Christian ethic smote my conscience, and I presented her with a rose – my inconsistency puzzling friend Joan. Strangely perhaps, the undisciplined behaviour was not instigated by the poorer scholarship girls, but mostly by those from the private prep, those whose parents were in the professional classes and who were born to lead.

Morning assembly for the whole school was held daily. It was presided over by the Head Mistress and included hymns or parts of hymns which I knew were not in keeping with Christadelphian belief. By that time, presumably, my parents considered I was old enough to withstand erroneous doctrines and I was therefore allowed to attend the assembly and also "stay in" for "Scripture" (whereas at St Mary's I had been withdrawn from the classes).

The instruction received bore little resemblance to the religious education of today. We had never heard of "multicultural faiths", "ethnic minorities" nor "racial equality", for those weren't contemporary issues. Britain had not yet

113

become a host nation. We rarely saw black or coloured people in our vicinity and when we did, though not aggressive toward them, we considered ourselves to be the superior white race who had built the triumphant British Empire. And, anyway, in Genesis the sons of Ham (presumed by some to be the blacks) had been cursed by God. Moreover Dr Thomas had not been averse to the use of slaves (their cruel exploitation still approved in Britain during his youth), for slavery had been condoned in both Old and New Testaments.

The comparatively few black people who were scattered in Britain during my childhood were highly sensitive to the inferiority with which they were generally regarded. One black gentleman asked Dad the name of a street, and was furious when he was told (correctly and with never an unkind thought) that it was Wightman Road. However, small girls lovingly nursed their black dolls (though I preferred white), and we delighted in the "golliwogs" without it ever occurring to us that black people might think we were belittling them.

In "Scripture" our teachers stuck firmly to the Authorised Version of the Bible. During part of my time at Hornsey High the headmistress taught our form. Miss Keating had only recently been appointed and the views she presented were, I suspect, much more in line with the Higher critics than were those of our more dignified Head, recently retired. Miss Keating was, we concluded, very modern and she amazed us by disregarding her dignity and even stepping on a chair to open a window!

Our former teacher of the subject had written on my report, "Ruth is not paying attention" – which presumably my parents would have thought was all to the good. And, anyway, I "knew it all" – so much better than the boring, non-disciplinarian, dithering Miss Dillon. But now that the Head took the lessons, I realised I had to pull up my lyle stockings, make sure their back seams were straight – and pay attention. I soon realised that she was hopelessly "astray". However, I deemed it diplomatic in the circumstances to keep my esoteric and superior knowledge to myself and made no effort to tackle so exalted a personage.

From time to time during my school career I was one of those unfortunates liable to be rendered helpless by fits of giggles which (even yet) are apt to affect youngsters – girls in particular. In the science lab giggles were scarcely conducive to directing iron filings or to the safe handling of a Bunsen burner. Plump Miss Elliott (who, on another occasion when presumably I was more deserving, kindly brought me a Christmas Rose to add to my pressed flower collection) hoped to bring me to my senses by imposing the punishment of learning the poem which commenced, "Life is real, life is earnest and the grave is not the goal...".

But once I had sobered up and recovered my equilibrium, I prided myself that Miss Ellis, who was, after all, a teacher of "science falsely so-called", was decidedly ignorant on the nature of the grave as compared to my superior self. Notwithstanding, I learned the poem, and once again diplomacy came to my aid and was deemed the better part of valour.

## A New Experience

At Hornsey High I acquired yet another "best friend". But she presented me with a most peculiar and hitherto unencountered problem. She, like myself, attended a small "meeting" with her parents. It was not of Christadelphian conviction and was composed almost entirely of relatives, but its members thought that they alone had "the Truth" and they alone were on the road to salvation. However, Marjorie seemed to be on much the same wave-length as myself in her manner of life, so her strange and very wrong conception of true religion did not disturb me unduly. I accepted the sincerity of her parents and that they thought that they were right. But, in contrast, I *knew* that it was *my* parents who understood "the Truth", and as none of the adults objected to our companionship we just accepted the puzzling impasse.

# A VISIT TO THE ZOO

On July 10th a party of fifth formers, accompanied by Miss Furniss and Miss Wilson, set out for the Zoo. We had hoped for bright weather, and we were disappointed though not surprised to find it raining after lunch. The weather was not too unkind, however, for when we arrived at the Zoo the sun was shining brightly.

We first visited the monkeys and watched with delight their peculiar antics. We next saw the tortoises and terrapins, and found them very sleepy after the lively monkeys. Then we went on to see the elephants and some of the party went for a joy-ride.

We hurried on to Mappin Terrace, and were just in time to see Barbara and Sam plunge for fish, giving us a shower bath. We walked along the terrace and saw the goats, who, although they appeared to be well fed, welcomed what we had to offer them—even attempting a guide book !

We then went to the Reptile House, and watched with fascinated horror as the snakes devoured their prey. We were very interested to see the results of experiments with different coloured lights on frogs' skins, which showed their adaptation to varied surroundings.

We had hoped to see the lions fed, but as we arrived a little too late, we fed ourselves and had tea at one of the refreshment houses. After tea we were fortunate enough to watch the sea-lions being fed. Some of us went to see the parrots, who seemed to take an instant dislike to us and screamed when we approached. One, however, differed from the rest, and even condescended to say "Hallo!"

At 5 o'clock we waited to watch the Chimpanzees' Tea Party. But alas ! the weather, as if it had forgotten itself in giving us a fine afternoon, made up for lost time. The rain came down in torrents, and we were soaked through, while the chimpanzees calmly continued with their tea.

We were very sorry when the time came for leaving the Zoo, for we had had such an enjoyable afternoon. We returned home a little weary, very wet—but not at all sad. We should like to thank all those who made such an afternoon possible, and we hope that Miss Furniss and Miss Wilson enjoyed the outing as much as we did.

RUTH WARD, Form VI (Commercial)
*Hornsey High School Magazine*, June 1937, pp, 20-21

116

# XIX
# "CHANGING SCENES OF LIFE"

In 1932 the lease of the rented Finsbury Park meeting hall was running out and it was decided to seek property to purchase. By then the reluctance to become owner-occupiers, in view of the expected return of Jesus Christ, was waning. Although the unrest among the nations apparently indicated his imminent return, it was realised that this had been so during the past seventy years of the Christadelphian community's existence. Further delay was still possible though not probable, but either way it was decided no harm could be done if the ecclesia were to purchase a hall. It would not perhaps be up to the architectural quality of the church buildings which we expected to take over in the kingdom, but could be useful, especially meantime. The urge to buy was strengthened by the fact that the members of the meeting, in common with their neighbours, were vacating their rented rooms, obtaining mortgages and buying the "electric" houses (as advertised) on the newly built suburban estates which were mushrooming on the outskirts of London and elsewhere. If members were possessing their own houses then as the prophet Haggai had indicated long ago, it seemed only right that attention should be paid to a house for God – which would be a Lightstand for "the Truth".

By the time I reached my twelfth birthday the ecclesia had acquired the ownership of a hall in Blackstock Road which thereafter attempted (and still attempts) to radiate its light. Now it seeks to attract not the almost entirely "white" population as then, but, as its address suitably suggests, the "blacks" who have since multiplied in the area following Britain's welcoming immigrants from the Empire after World War II so that they could take over the surplus of low-paid, menial jobs. The hall was soon registered for marriage services which enabled couples to be joined in marriage by a Brother despite Dr Thomas' view that any such service savoured of

117

"priestcraft", and that marriage should be entered into only by a civil ceremony. The ecclesia was able to lend the hall to surrounding Christadelphian meetings, and this helped to prevent couples from hiring a church building for the ceremony, a practice which was currently being deplored in *The Christadelphian*.

## Wedding at Finsbury Park Meeting Room of Ken Jones and Rosemary Grantham (Ruth's cousin), March 1951

*Left to right:* **Jack Ward, John Ward, Eunice Cook, Marion Cook with daughter Gillian, Denis Cook, Ruth McHaffie with Peter (16 months), George McHaffie, Gwladys Ward ... Enid Grantham (bridesmaid) with Ian (aged 5) and David (aged 4), Ken & Rosemary Jones, May Ward, Syd Grantham (at back), Gladys Grantham ....**

John, by then sixteen, had for some time walked a few steps behind or in front of the family as we walked uphill and down again to the meeting. This manner of progression was not altogether novel for (unknown to John) it had been the custom of Robert Roberts to walk separately from his wife, Jane, en route to the Sunday services, his purpose being to enable him to concentrate on his duties for the day. John's reason was rather less worthy and we presumed that as a "big

118

boy" he was reluctant to be seen by any peers accompanied by his parents. Moreover he soon rebelled against attending the evening lectures, and was allowed to stay at home on condition that he didn't go out to play. Whether John "played cricket" in our absence we never knew.

Suddenly, however, it was all change. He, together with asserting independence, fell into line and became the first candidate to be baptised at the new premises in the meeting's own bath under the platform. This event both pleased and alarmed Mum and Dad who were fearful that at the age of sixteen, he did not understand the seriousness of the step he was taking. Robert Robert's son, Edward, had pleased his parents by being baptised when he was fifteen – but he had not stayed the course. However John was not to be stopped and his youthful enthusiasm was soon channelled into giving addresses at the Mutual Improvement Society's classes, and he proudly wore one of the popular enamelled Mutual Improvement Society's badges.

(*Finsbury Park*).—As intimated in our report last month, we held the first services in our new hall on Sept. 11th. It was with feelings of thankfulness to our heavenly Father for granting us the privilege of being able to possess our own hall that we assembled together. Hitherto, as many readers are aware, we have been compelled to restrict ourselves to meeting on Sundays and Wednesdays only in a hired room, but now, if the need arises, we can meet at any time. A list of the meetings so far arranged to take place weekly is to be found on the back page. On Wednesday, Sept. 22nd, before a number of brethren and sisters, Mr. John Ward (son of our Bro. and Sister Ward, and grandson of Bro. and Sister Sparkhall, was baptised into the saving name of Christ. He received the right hand of fellowship on Sunday, Sept. 25th. We earnestly entreat our brother to remain "pure in the doctrine and strong in the word " to the end of his life and so merit the permanent possession of the mantle of salvation lent him at his immersion.

*Fraternal Visitor,*
**October 1932**

One Wednesday evening he gave a talk which, if I remember correctly, was on spiritualism. Those were the days when young speakers received sharp criticism at the classes so as to improve their performances on the platforms. George Alcock (to whom we were so indebted for our seaside holidays) did not mince his words. To my mother's horror John, after his conscientious effort, was told that his essay was not worth the paper it was written on (though afterwards Brother Alcock apologised for being so harsh). Few of the young today would accept the criticisms made in times past. But then it was a case of "let nothing you dismay", and a respected senior Brother would have been referred to as "dear Brother Bloggs" and not as "old Jo". But, anyway, Mum and Dad need not have worried over John's early start nor the criticism received, for more than sixty years later and until the end of his life, he remained "pure in the doctrine and strong in the Word". And perhaps it was those early disciplinary exercises which ensured that in his dying months after a stroke, he was still struggling to provide his (by then dependent) ecclesia with a mid-week address recorded in hospital.

John Ward and Ruth Ward, Easter 1939,
at the Arley Castle Christadelphian Conference, Bewdly.
Ruth is wearing her Hornsey High School blazer.

# XX
# OUT OF THE ARCHIVES

With Dad often being at work and John having become an independent attender there were times when Mum and I walked alone, and this provided an excellent opportunity for her to tell me something of her early life and to impart important information to the best of her ability.

She had been glad to leave school at fourteen (in 1902) for she found the teachers frightening which was not surprising since they had to be stern disciplinarians in order to cope with about seventy children in each class. But "going out to work" provided little improvement. She was at first employed in her grumpy father's second-hand furniture shop, relieving her boredom, when Grandad wasn't looking, by reading under the counter. That particular business venture was short-lived and she then moved into a dressmaking establishment with its long hours and dismal conditions.

## Glad Tidings

Suddenly the sun shone – with the arrival of the firm's buttons, delivered by a very respectable young Salvationist (referred to earlier). Before long a friendship developed between them and because the Sunday dinner-pot at home had none to spare, she shared her portion with him, and when he brought her a bunch of flowers she, unaccustomed to receiving such personal attention, was so embarrassed she hid them behind the piano. Together they went along to the young people's Sunday Afternoon Class held at the meeting room – and *so* enjoyed the tea, which wasn't surprising after having only half a dinner. Sometimes they also went to the P.S.A. (Pleasant Sunday Afternoons) which were run by a group trying to encourage young people to behave well and to think on serious matters, and which we might think was a suitable venue. But *The Fraternal Visitor* magazine had no sympathy for any such movement and described it as "one of the religious fashions of the day". It was "a reflection on the prevailing shallowness which characterises society in an increasing degree".[31] Studying only "the Truth" was considered to be of any value. My parents were no youthful rebels but the editor who was so condemnatory was not among those who experienced the hardships of the poorer classes. He apparently lacked the ability to understand the need there was for a respectable couple to have "somewhere nice" to spend an hour or so.

The Afternoon Class held at the meeting hall was conducted by Brother H. H. Horsman. He was regarded as a wonderful leader of high standing. It was with the help of his influence that Dad "came in". But then, so I was told, and unbelievably, Brother Horsman had "gone astray" and "left the Truth".

LONDON (*Finsbury Park*).—It is with much pleasure we report a further addition to our number by the baptism, on Oct. 2nd, of Mr. J. F. Ward (19), formerly of the Salvation Army. This is a further testimony to the good work which is being done by our Sunday afternoon class, of which he was a member; and we trust that the efforts there put forth will be further blessed.

How such an appalling thing could have happened was beyond my understanding. No explanation was given me, and perhaps I was too shocked to ask. But one day I would understand. And how delighted my mother would have been had she known that when the centenary issue of *Glad Tidings* would be issued in the 1980s, Brother Horsman's article which had taken the lead in its first issue would be reprinted, given pride of place once more (the editor presumably unaware of his "heretical" history?). And by then, many in the Brotherhood (though to the deep disapproval of the *Glad Tidings* publishers) would go a long way in agreeing with the disgraced stalwart – as explained in my companion volume, *Reformation and Renewal*.

## "Be not conformed to this world"

There were lighter and less puzzling stories related to me during our walking to the meeting. Mum recalled the shock which went through the meeting when a fashion-conscious

---

[31] *The Fraternal Visitor*, May 1898, p. 148

sister arrived with her hair "bobbed". Other Sisters soon followed suit, had their long locks cut, and adopted one or other of the new worldly "hair-do's" – either a "bob" or a "shingle". Some, uncertain of the permissibility of following the new trend, wrote to the editor for advice. In his reply Charles Walker quoted from the apostle Paul in 1 Corinthians 11, apparently thinking that would "cut short" the intrusive modernity.[32] There were, of course, many outside the Brotherhood who were appalled at the new hair styles. In 1926 the press reported that one father of a young unmarried daughter was so angry when she had her hair bobbed, that she feared to return to the house again and drowned herself, leaving her father distraught with grief.

Mum knew nothing of "going to the hairdresser" and she kept to the traditional length. Dad loved her (early greyed) hair as much as he loved her, and her having it shortened or wearing any make-up on her face (which he considered was after the manner of Jezebel) would have grieved him deeply. I, too, was never taken to any hair salon but I was allowed to have a "bob", cut and styled at home.

Eventually Charles Walker (and other conservatives) proved no more able to hold back the new styles than had John Thomas been able to prevent male members from adopting updated styles in their appearances. Our pioneer was convinced that the "gravity, heroism, dignity and excellence of the ancient world are with the beard", "the symbol of manly thought and action uncontrolled by human imbecility" but "the levity, effeminacy, dandyism and servility of all ages with the smooth-faced shaveling of ignoble mien".[33] Dad, like some other Brethren who apparently were reluctant to go the whole-hog, went halfway, and retained his moustache, though over the rest of his face he adopted "human imbecility" by employing his shaving brush, soap-stick, and cut-throat razor – using his leather strop for sharpening it.

---

[32] *The Christadelphian*, September 1933, p. 406

[33] *The Christadelphian*, September 1892, pp. 322-323

123

Other shock waves were soon to run through the ecclesias, this time of the permanent variety. Sisters, to whom nature had communicated in no uncertain terms that their hair was intended to be long, straight and even lanky, not only had their natural "coverings" lopped but had the remainders set in "permanent" corrugations. Gone were the curls made overnight with rags or tongs heated on gas ring or coalfire. Now the hairdresser had taken over in no small way. American-style lipstick, rouge and eye shadow were added as well as the face powder. And horror of horrors! One Sister who stays fixed in my shocked mind's eye even dyed her hair! My parents were appalled, and therefore so was I. But things change (don't they just?) and one consolation for our present day community is that the now common use of dyes in all their attractive shades will prevent it from being too noticeable that we, in Britain, are composed largely of "greys".

By the 1920/30s the charming flower and fruit holders, the plates and the caskets which had been balanced delicately on the heads of our earlier Sisters (blocking members' views of the speaking Brethren) had been replaced by the flower-pot "cloches". These latest fashion pieces, with or without rims and with or without flowers, still preserved the gardening theme though were not nearly so pretty. A Mr David Thompson writing on *Nonconformity in the Nineteenth Century* had remarked on the colourfulness of the congregation of some five thousand at the Metropolitan Tabernacle in 1878, those who flocked to hear Dwight Moody's preaching and David Sankey's singing accompanied by his small reed organ. Christadelphians have always been exhorted to wear modest apparel but have never lagged far behind in keeping up with the trends of fashion. Thompson's description of the Tabernacle congregation would have applied to our community's gatherings (on a smaller scale) as evidenced by old photos, black and white though they are. "Looking down from the height at which we sit", he wrote, "the great number of bright-coloured hats and bonnets of the women on the floor of the house look like a parterre of flowers, and higher up, the first tier, sloping from the back to the front, presents the appearance of flowers on a vast stand".

124

Alas, I was born too late to enjoy such beauty, and by my time even the grand ostrich feathers had disappeared from ladies' head-gear, together with the discontinuance of adverts on the covers of *The Christadelphian* by Sisters who earned their daily bread fashioning them artistically. But at least that was one of the changes in fashion which proved to be an advantage, for women's vanity had rendered the poor ostrich an endangered species.

Finsbury Park Ecclesial Outing to Hadley Woods,
14 August 1909 – Jack Ward in middle row, third from left.

**"Where did you come from, Baby dear?"**

Like all Christadelphians, my mother was well geared to the idea of "special efforts". But she was determined to make one specifically for my benefit. And going to the meeting again provided the opportunity. When she herself had matured into a teenager she was altogether ignorant of the functioning of the human body. Despite all the babies born (and dying) in the neighbourhood round about her, she knew nothing of menstruation and at her first period she was so frightened she thought she was dying. Grannie was a kind and caring mother and her inability to explain the facts of life to her daughters was merely in keeping with her

125

contemporaries' embarrassment both in "the Truth" and out of it. Sex and everything related to it was taboo. Nor had much change been made by my own day, although there was some enlightenment for those of us who enjoyed biology in our secondary education. But even then the teaching was more by implication rather than by any kind of sex education. The word itself was seldom used – a sharp contrast today when it is taken out of context, and a hyped-up official document is described, quite absurdly, as being "sexed up".

Mum obviously had difficulty in wording her explanations and I was left to draw conclusions for myself, which led to some strange misconceptions. When I was enthusing to her about spawning frogs (at school) she took the opportunity of commenting that "humans are like that". She must have made quite an impression for I remember clearly the very spot as we crossed the road by Crouch End clocktower, where such fascinating information was imparted. She also told me of mothers having babies they didn't want. This was exceedingly puzzling – for how could anyone not want so miraculous a possession? And, anyway, if a baby was unwanted why did a couple not desist from behaving "like frogs"?

That sex in itself could be, for some, an uncontrollable urge was only hinted. But I was to hear more. Mum told me of the kind Marie Stopes who (despite reaping loud condemnation, in particular from church dignitaries) had recently opened a clinic devoted to helping the prevention of unwanted births, and how someone she knew well had been greatly helped by her. I think the words "birth control" were never mentioned, perhaps because my mother didn't know them. Somehow, however, I realised the need for caution and, absurdly, was just a little afraid when a gentleman sitting beside me in the bus put his hand on my knee (intentionally or unintentionally) that I might be going to have a baby. Nor could I understand Mum's wrath when I told her that a well-known visitor who happened to be alone with me in the kitchen for a few minutes was so kind and endearing, and kissed me so much. There simply seemed to be no accounting for the peculiar behaviour and reactions of grown-ups.

126

But at least I gathered that I was not to pause and look in the windows of certain shops (despite their apparently respectable exteriors), and into my late teens I thought birth control was the controlling of whether or not a boy or a girl was born. I had no idea of the extent of the problems which many women suffered and not only those in the world, for Brethren and Sisters were every bit as prolific as "outsiders" in "replenishing the earth". I was totally unaware that there could ever have been written any letter such as one of many received by Marie Stopes when I was almost a year old in 1921,

> What I would like to know is how can I save having more children as I think I have done my duty by my country having 13 children.... I have 6 boys alive now and a little girl who will be 3 years old in May. I buried a dear little baby girl three weeks old who died from the strain of whooping cough. I have not had much time for pleasure and it is telling on me now I suffer very bad from varicose veins in my legs and my ankles gives out and I just drops down. I am please to tell you that I received one of those willow plates from the News of the World for mothers of ten [sic].[34]

Why, when I was a teenager, I was so dim that I didn't ask for more information remains puzzling. But as my practical daughter frequently reminds me when I bemoan my many past deficiencies, "It's too late to be worrying about that *now!*". But it's never too late to learn (is it?) and one of my granddaughters has been kind enough to update me on the subject, together with other matters which have eluded me. And despite the exaggerated emphasis which modern society places on sex, how good it is that one generation can discuss freely with another, with none of the taboos which used to be in force!

As far as I am aware, no comments were made on the unmentionable subject of birth control by anyone in the Christadelphian community, and it was a great surprise when

---

[34] Beddoe, *Back to Home and Duty*, p. 105

in my early twenties in the 1940s a colleague told me that Christadelphians didn't believe in birth control – so surprised, in fact, that I never thought to ask how she knew. Looking back it can be observed that whatever the official line of the community (if one existed) she was wrong, for members had mostly taken the law into their own hands, and by one method or another had stopped having large families, as had also the second and third editors of *The Christadelphian*. In the 1960s one well-known Brother had intended to include advice on birth control in a booklet on marriage he had been commissioned to write, but his intention was thwarted by the hierarchy. Possibly it was not "nice" enough for our community reading, and like the zealous millennialist of the 17th century it was believed, "God's Scholars ... are [only] perfected with learning from above". Sadly, Christadelphia's main concern for maturing girls in our sex-obsessed world of the 21st century seems to centre, not on sensible advice on the subject, but on emphasising how because of Eve's conduct in Eden their voices in our community must not be heard in spiritual devotions, however aged and/or inadequate the ecclesia's Brethren.

In "outside" upper class families the birth rate had been falling since the 1870s, which indicated that some form of control (though most often without the use of rudimentary mechanical devices) was being used. Abstinence provided the solution for some, but prostitutes provided it for others, often wrecking the lives of poverty-stricken girls with unwanted pregnancies and venereal disease. By the 1920s birth control of some kind was being exercised in our community which was, undoubtedly, an advantage for child-bearing Sisters, but not for the growth of Christadelphia. As the years have passed, not only has its "nursery" seen fewer occupants, but also many now nurtured "within" are abandoning "the Truth". This could be seen as a warning that something is lacking in our community. But many would think it merely a sign of the Last Day which it is believed would be preceded by a fall-away. If larger families brought into the world in recent years would have meant merely a larger number of lapsees (estimated I am told at three out of four), we cannot tell.

# XXI
# OVERCAST SKIES

For some years Christadelphians (in particular) had been aware during the years of my secondary schooldays, of the anxiety felt by the Jews in Germany, numbering about half a million. In March 1933 *The Christadelphian* had quoted Herr Hitler declaring that his policy included "as its first point to live in peace and friendship with all countries", but it was known, nevertheless, that the Jews were among those being made scapegoats for Germany's defeat in the Great War and for the economic depression which had followed. World leaders and perceptive Europeans were deeply worried. Charles Walker had commented at the beginning of that year, "...the world is on the brink of the abyss". But I, personally, was then at the stage when I preferred the authorship of Angela Brazil and her schoolgirl adventures to reading anything that Charles Walker had to say. And the attitude of neighbouring Londoners was not one of alarm. They were not unduly disturbed by Hitler's activities, nor by any persecution of the Jews. Hitler was seen by many in Britain as a genius to be admired for he was putting his homeland back on her feet. Perhaps there were gross exaggerations in the newspapers, and, anyway, many of the British didn't care much for Jews.

Working class people at that time seldom travelled abroad. Those who could rise to hard-earned holidays still went mostly by bus or train to Britain's popular seaside resorts. But some of the girls at school did go to the Continent, usually accompanied by their parents or on one of the school trips which the privileged could afford.

One of our Sixth Formers visited Germany in 1933, just after Hitler had come into power. Friends thought she might be taking a risk in travelling to Germany unaccompanied, and, she wrote flippantly in the school magazine, "Some even offered to subscribe to my ransom if I were sent to a concentration camp!"

Her account of the visit proved reassuring. Fears, she explained, were unfounded. Walking down the High Street in Bonn seemed no different from walking down Crouch End Broadway except that one met numerous Brownshirts and Storm Troopers. Some English people seemed to imagine that there was a Nazi in an invisible cloak listening to everyone's conversation and waiting to make arrests at the slightest provocation. She found it interesting that the children were "educated to think Fascism by being given not baby dolls but Nazi dolls, not tin soldiers but tin Nazis...". When she had travelled through the country lanes and villages in a charabanc, she noticed that the children they passed, instead of waving, had given the Fascist salute. Nearly every motor car and bicycle was flying a small swastika flag. Necklaces, bracelets, brooches and rings bore the same symbol. Instead of saying "Good morning" the greeting had become "Heil Hitler" for though Hitler had only been "in power less than a year, everybody from the smallest child to the oldest inhabitant seemed to believe that his policy alone could bring back happiness and prosperity to their native land".[35]

The ever increasing victimisation of the Jewish population seems to have remained unseen by many a visitor, but in March of that same year the *Daily Mail* had reported that "The boycott of the Jews is to begin in every town and village in Germany on Saturday 'at 10 a.m. sharp'". In some places it had already begun. Jewish shops had been forcibly closed and windows smeared with tar.[36]

The major economies of the world were by then in trouble, though Stalin was adding military strength to the formidable Russia. In 1934, Germany, which had been allowed to join the League of Nations in 1926, made an ominous move by withdrawing from it. In the same year, with his power rising, Hitler attempted to annex Austria to

---

[35] "A Visit to Germany", Ruth Page, *Hornsey High School Magazine*, March 1934, pp. 32-33

[36] *The Christadelphian*, May 1933, p. 221

Germany, though his move proved abortive. But in the following January, he contrived by intrigue to gain a 90% majority vote in the Saar for re-union with Germany. Two months later he not only re-introduced conscription but let the world know that he was building up Germany's military strength. That he thought nothing of treaty breaking was becoming obvious but both the British and French governments were economically and politically unprepared for war and did nothing to protest. In October of the same year, Italy under Mussolini attacked Abyssinia and began to befriend Hitler, and in 1935 Japan was steadily extending its invasion into China. Military dictatorships were on the march.

All these developments were watched with eagle eyes by the Christadelphian community. The seventh vial of the book of Revelation which was to be poured out "into the air" was by many in our community now thought to have a literal interpretation, differing from Dr Thomas' figurative exposition. It was considered that during the 1914-18 war the 'pouring out' had begun, with bombs being dropped from aircraft. Before long it would be completed in the huge conflict which was about to destroy the ungodly.

**Remains of a bomb dropped in Edinburgh, by a German Zeppelin airship, April 1916.**

131

Meanwhile, in the summer of 1935, the British with patriotic fervour were celebrating the Jubilee of King George V and Queen Mary. Boisterous street parties were held with rousing jollifications, flags and banners. We were all given a day's holiday from school, and though I attended no party, I was pleased with my gift of a commemorative mug and enjoyed collecting acorns under the old oak tree in the park.

Eight months later our beloved King died, and the celebrations changed to mourning. There was more pomp and ceremony, though this time of sombre character. Nations, however, soon recover from mourning a dead king, and Edward, Prince of Wales, was readily welcomed as the new monarch. Many were the wishes that long might he live for he had made himself popular with the people. His handsome and dashing appearance had ensured that young ladies fell for his charm, and working girls pinned up his photo. In 1920 he "received a right royal welcome home" after his great Empire tour, and Christadelphian readers were told that "his cheery exhortation to 'Pull together' can do no harm at any rate". During his tour in 1919, he had been presented by the Jewish citizens at Montreal with a tablet of gold on which the Ten Commandments were inscribed in Hebrew.[37] He seemed to make an effort to show concern for his "neighbour" during the depression of the 1930s when he visited those in affected areas and won popularity, even if nothing was done to alleviate their misery.

But in 1936 disaster struck and there was a constitutional crisis, since recorded at length in the history books and discussed over and over again on the media. At the time Fleet Street exercised suitable restraint as requested, and the new King's intention to marry Mrs Wallis Simpson, who was in the process of divorcing her second husband, was kept quiet for as long as possible. But eventually his determination to proceed with the marriage had to be made known to us. Britain was horrified. The coronation could not go ahead. News placards thereafter blazed with the latest developments, and wireless bulletins were awaited with baited breath. It was all so much more interesting than boring information about

---

[37] *The Christadelphian*, December 1919, p. 556

military dictatorships and the problems of the Jews. At the end of the year, on 11th December, I leaned on our sideboard in the kitchen at Palace Road (our home address suitably matching the royal occasion) and joined the millions who listened to the King's emotional abdication address and his declaration that he could never occupy the throne "without the woman I love".

The whole affair was not so distressing to the Christadelphians as it was to many of the King's subjects, though his marriage to a woman twice (or even once) divorced could not be condoned. Henry VIII might have behaved outrageously with his successive queens, though he had – temporarily, at least – rid England of Rome, the "Scarlet Woman". But that a member of our devout and beloved royal family could behave so badly was shocking indeed. It was one of those occasions when it was right for us to ignore the scriptural precept that we should "honour the king". Although we had been disappointed that Victoria, Edward VII and George V had all passed from history without the opportunity of yielding the British crown to Christ, yet God was ruling in the kingdom of men, and Edward could never have been destined to be King. It was fitting, therefore, that his younger brother, George, should take the throne, and that he, together with his charming wife and two delightful little daughters, should become the focus of public attention.

The new royal family was taken to the heart of the nation and the Empire. In 1937 the Coronation with all its splendour took place in Westminster Abbey. Our Middlesex schools were allotted seats and we were suitably represented by our Head Girl, while representatives of each form in the school went to the Town Hall to hear the Proclamation of the King's Accession. It all went off "with many a banner flaunted and sound of trumpet and drum" as Elise Hood in Form IV poetically described the event in the school magazine.[38]

---

[38] "Westminster Abbey at Coronation" by Elise Hood, *Hornsey High School Magazine*, June 1937, p. 49

Düsseldorf residents greet German troops during the occupation of the Rhineland (March 10, 1936). This was a deliberate breach by Hitler of the treaty of Versailles which had aimed to keep the Rhineland as a demilitarized buffer zone between Germany and France.

# XXII
# APPROACHING DOOM

While our powers-that-were had been occupied with so unexpected a turn in constitutional affairs, in Europe events were increasingly threatening. While Britain was busy with the Coronation, Adolf Hitler took advantage to progress his treaty-breaking and sent troops into the Rhineland. The same year saw the beginning of the Spanish Civil War. When in 1930 we had marvelled at Amy Johnson's feat of flying solo from Croydon to Darwin in nineteen-and-a-half days, we had no conception of the horrors which would result from the advances in aviation. But the terrifying consequences of warfare in the air became apparent during the conflict in Spain when their Civil War offered useful practice to other Europeans for the widespread aerial combat soon to follow.

The last thing the British people wanted was another war. There were still too many ghastly memories of the previous one, too many people still suffering from its effects. Various efforts were made to encourage people to think peace. At school we had a branch of the "League of Nations Union". The meetings were held after school. There would be tea, then girls in the Sixth Form would give papers on the objects and activities of the League, followed by games, perhaps a charade on disarmament and (in late 1936) a lecture was given by a Mr Wilson on "Palestine" and the "present-day acute problems of government" there owing to the "contrasting modes of life of the Arabs and the Jewish immigrants".

There was, of course, never any question of my joining the Union or attending its meetings. Christadelphians did not look for international peace but for international war. That the Jews were being persecuted was the judgment of God because of their disobedience. Hitler, it was thought, had been raised up to incite increasing persecution so that the Jews would be driven back to Palestine, and though few of us were aware of it, Zionists were negotiating with him in order to boost the "return" of the Jews. So far as our community was concerned, that many had fled or committed suicide was all a sign of the times, a sign that the End was fast approaching. The gentleman, Mr Wilson, who addressed the girls at Hornsey High was, of course, unaware of any such interpretation of events, but the lecture he gave would not have been deemed profitable by my parents for my spiritual education.

In August 1936, the Olympic Games were held in Germany with lavish extravaganza. To avoid catching the eye of foreign visitors, notices indicating that the Jews were not welcome were removed from the surrounding areas. The peoples of Britain and Germany were still friends. At Easter in 1937 a group of thirty one girls, with our Headmistress and four members of staff set out for a holiday in Germany. As the "Members of the Party" later reported in the magazine, they had a wonderful time, welcomed on all sides by the Germans. As one old gentleman put it, "By jove, by jingo, good gracious, what have we here? English young ladies, ja?". At Cologne they were pleasantly surprised to find in the dining room "little pots of flowers set before each place and the German flag and the Union Jack placed on each table". As every tourist did, they explored the sights, ancient and modern of one fascinating city after another. In Munich the guide pointed out the building where Hitler first began his campaign in 1919; they observed the four soldiers always on duty guarding a stone erected to the memory of sixteen members of his party who had been killed in the 1923 uprising, and they saw the Braunes Haus, the headquarters of the Nazi movement in Southern Bavaria. They were enthralled by the Deutsches Museum, "the largest science museum in the world". And, finally, they left for home, intending "to return some day".[39]

And perhaps they would, but not for many years. Who could imagine the horrific destruction which would soon rain down on that "delightful country" with its charming and quaint buildings, nor the onslaught which would obliterate

---

[39] "German Holiday, Easter, 1936", *Hornsey High School Magazine*, June 1937, pp. 27-34

the brightly coloured market stalls, and those who had filled them with colour. In Cologne the "little pots of flowers set before each place" with the "the German flag and the Union Jack" side by side would be blown off the map. The city would suffer the terrifying onslaught of saturation bombing when 1000 Royal Air Force planes would raid it. Yet, looking back at our school magazine, there is something uncannily ominous in the comment, "...the sky became overcast once more, and as we approached Munich we drove through a blizzard—we had left the sunshine in the mountains".

# Headquarters of The Post Office Savings Bank

**Blythe House, West Kensington,
where Ruth was first employed.**
Photo by courtesy of Docben, Creative Commons Attribution
http://en.wikipedia.org/wiki/Blythe_House

# XXIII
# TIME TO GROW UP

By now, the time had come for me to leave school. No longer would I march into morning prayers in time to Miss McAuliffe's stirring rendering of the *Trumpet Voluntary*, and no longer would I sing about building Jerusalem in England's green and pleasant land. As in the words of the oft repeated Anglican (and school) prayer I had 'read, learned and inwardly digested' at least some of the information which Hornsey High had offered, and had received "my bow of burning gold" in the form of a sound education thanks to the patience of the staff. Importantly, I had acquired a reasonably acceptable way of expressing myself, for speaking BBC English and avoiding regional accents was important. As a college student (in the 1940s) was quoted saying, "I don't remember anybody without the right accent doing well". But the financial situation at home determined that there was no possibility of my moving into full-time further education. So I, now "Miss Ward", had to step out with dignity into the formal world and face the evils of which I had been so often warned.

My solo journeyings, or those with cousins or a friend, had until then been confined to our own neighbourhood. On being accepted into the Civil Service, I hoped to be placed in a relatively local office. Instead I was planted in West Kensington and to my initial horror had to travel six days of the week underground from one end of London to the other, with Saturdays being only a half-holiday in keeping with the then normal working pattern. The tedium of these journeys was relieved by most passengers with their reading (as still today), and I soon did likewise. Oddly, the only piece of information which I remember absorbing in the process, is Islip Collyer's observation to the effect (if I remember rightly) that if you had a struggle in fixing the stud in your shirt's collar, it was useless getting angry with the stud. As one of the frailer gender, I had, of course, no stud-fixing problem but I did realise the applicability of his point to many of life's vexations.

My destination, the Post Office Savings Bank, was the most boring place imaginable. Since for so long I had been in a single-sex school, it would be reasonable to suppose that my placement would have seemed familiar and homely, for the lady-like supervisors were strict but quite amiable, and colleagues were friendly. But the very vastness of it all was off-putting, and I was terribly afraid of making mistakes. But though, in common with many of my peers, I lacked the confidence of so many young people today, the idea of abandoning the job never occurred to me. Going out to work was a serious business and to give up was not an option, however unnerving or boring the exercise.

**Female clerks in the 1930s operate adding machines to prepare daily balances at the Post Office Savings Bank, Blythe House, West Kensington**

Photo: United Kingdom Government – Public Domain

The Savings Bank in earlier days had been strictly divided into men's and women's branches, but integration was on the move when my career started. The Civil Service, as compared with many other employers was, even then, caring for the welfare of its staff with medical checks. For some reason "Establishment" (the personnel section) soon transferred me to a "men's branch", as it was still called. Possibly I was moved because, as the Medical Officer told me, I was in some way, a square peg in a round hole. How different it all was! When God decided it was not good for man to be alone, He created a principle for all time. Men and women need the balance of one other. The new branch was even bigger than the previous one – so big that it was scarcely possible to see from one end of the room to the other. But the few girls in it formed a happy little group bunched in the middle and the gentlemen (for gentle men they were) seemed to lack the deplorable worldliness I had expected, and (with hindsight) were kindly encouraging and tolerant of my lack of maturity and sophistication. On reflection I perceive they were mildly amused, with one telling me I ought still to be at school. This new placement in the "Stock Branch" operated the buying and selling by investors of their "consols" and "bonds" or whatever government shares they held. The work had to be done in keeping with the rules and timing of the Stock Exchange which meant that there was a stimulating "crisis" every day. From then on I realised that having to work to a deadline (on whatever task) makes for efficiency, achievement and job satisfaction.

I soon perceived, as was inevitable, that most other girls had a worldliness which I lacked. Their ball-room dancing, cinema and theatre-going, their make-up and their "young men" were in sharp contrast to anything I knew. But listening to their conversations was an education in itself, and they were friendly even though they must have thought me an out-dated oddity. Although I didn't appreciate it at the time, by comparison with my Grannie who had to go into domestic service, and my mother who had to work appallingly long hours in the dress-making firm, together with poor conditions, I was highly privileged. Through the influence of educationalists and social reformers, and when parents such as my own could and would co-operate, the child from the working class family was given the opportunity of avoiding life at the bottom of the heap. Though I had received no specific training, yet I had enough education to build on and which ensured that I was launched into a working life where conditions of service were strictly controlled and where exploitation didn't exist.

In the early days of Christadelphia, education and training other than of an elementary nature had been discouraged. Christ was at the door and the only learning needed was "the Truth". Dr Thomas despised universities and would have agreed heartily with Brother Grahame Cooper who more recently informed his readers that "Theology, as served up to modern man by the joint forces of Church and University" is "poisonous fare".[40] But Islip Collyer (whom I never met but who wrote some of the most balanced statements published in Christadelphian literature) produced an article entitled *The Day of His Coming*. Referring to his own former years (at the end of the 19th and beginning of the 20th centuries) he wrote,

> The expectation that the end was near not only revealed itself in our conversation, but in our attitude toward life. It did not seem worth while to make any preparation for living in the kingdoms of men as they were practically ended, so some of the young people were well grounded in the scriptures but not trained for anything in the world. Then later, when they discovered that they were ordinary human beings after all with human needs and wants, and when circumstances turned them out of the parental home, they discovered that the world was a very cruel workshop for untrained men.

I was never in the unhappy position of having to leave the parental home before I chose to do so. From birth, naturally, I had been provided for and as I pursued the slippery path of youth it never occurred to me that had I left school at fourteen, as most of my contemporaries did, then I would

---

[40] *Glad Tidings*, No 1325, p. 12

have stood less chance of being placed in so sheltered an environment once I had to face the world. Nor did it ever occur to me that had I left school sooner I could have made a contribution to the limited family income. Parental sacrifice and care were simply taken for granted. The same loving parental devotion is still frequently given today, and often is still received unacknowledged. Perhaps the difference between then and now is that present-day parents are so much more affluent and are usually giving of their comparative plenty.

## Farewell to Grannie

At the beginning of the 21st century we are all familiar with the idea of the elderly "going into care". But in earlier times grannies and grandads were mostly cared for by their families once they became too frail to be independent, and provision for their needs by the state was skeletal. Grannie developed glaucoma together with other problems. In the absence of early detection and the treatment which usually now controls that eye condition, she lost her sight and suffered considerable pain.

In the last three weeks of her life she, who had so loved our garden, was in great distress because she thought we had left her there. Small and frail as she was, Dad was able to carry her round the house hoping to convince her that we had brought her inside, but it was a blessing when at last she rested "in the bosom of her Father and her God".

Grannie Sparkhall
née Sarah Hatton
(1858-1938)

It was customary when a death occurred for the venetian blinds to be lowered on the front windows. Neighbours would take note and lower theirs too. Women seldom attended funerals, and so, though I was provided with a little mauve dress by way of mourning, I stayed at home with my mother to prepare a meal for family visitors on their return from the cemetery. And as my lavender-scented friend was borne away I had peered through the blinds, knowing that as the cortege moved along the streets, the passers-by would stand still as a mark of respect and the gentlemen would take off their hats. Modest grandeur though it was, it was more than Grannie had ever known during her lifetime.

# XXIV
# "IN THE BUD
# OF EARLY SPRINGTIME"

When I was in my teens I was sometimes invited to one or other of the "speaking" Brethren's privately owned residences, often situated in the new housing estates. Their grand name plates, "Maranatha" ("May the Lord come"), for example, and their modern bathrooms, electrical contrivances, and even a telephone, compared startlingly with our arrangements at home. Many of them had moved up from working to middle class, as unknowingly, we too were gradually moving.

I admired their "lawn" (we only had "grass"), enjoyed the "lunch" (we only had "dinner"), was most impressed that they even had a splendid cut-glass jug filled with water and glass tumblers to match, artistically displayed on the white damask table cloth. My culinary vocabulary was distinctly limited, so when asked if I liked Welsh Rabbit, I could only reply "Well, we don't have rabbit at home". Anyway, I knew to tread gingerly on their deep-piled, carpets, and perched myself amid the rouched satin cushions on their posh "sofas" (we only had a "couch"), speaking when I was spoken to. I admired their decor and ornaments and hoped that one day (though I was uncertain quite how) I might acquire at least one pink and white infant like the portrait by Bessie Pease Gutmann which hung on the wall of one (unavoidably childless) couple.

As today, some, with their wives, made outstanding contributions to the encouragement of the young. Cyril and Mary Cooper, in particular, kept an open house. Having no family of their own they "parented" any in the ecclesias who needed their help, even hosting a wedding reception, as well as encouraging those who had no special needs. At Easter they arranged a ramble which preceded the Watford ecclesial annual "Fraternal", both events eagerly attended. Contemporaries (declining in number) will also recall with happy memories the Arley Castle House parties at Bewdley, which Cyril and Mary, bounding with enthusiasm, organised at Easter time prior to the outbreak of World War II. Not only did the company of other young people delight us but the beautiful grounds of the Castle gladdened our hearts "in the bud of early Springtime". After the war the organising of the event was taken over by my brother John and his wife Gwladys, and they likewise, having no family of their own, used their energies to help the offspring of others.

Some years later Mary Cooper died unexpectedly and prematurely during an operation. Those of us who knew her still remember her as an outstandingly vigorous Sister. Her husband, Cyril, lived sufficiently long for him to enter the Christadelphian Nursing Home as a frail old Brother whose mind had failed. The young staff who cared for him would remember him only as such and would have found it hard to imagine his earlier strength, vitality and enthusiasm. They would know nothing of the deep respect we felt for him, the city Bank Manager, as he organised us and so much else long before. In earlier days and before the Welfare State came into existence, elderly people did not linger on in life, repeatedly bolstered up by medication, as so many of us do today. But that was not the disadvantage which some younger people might think, for the time often arrives when as the writer of Ecclesiastes observed, the aged feel (albeit still smiling for the benefit of relatives) that they "have no pleasure in them" or their enjoyment of life is much diminished.

I am reminded of once reading the advice to young people caring for the elderly that they should try to realise that a frail, decrepit old lady might well once have been the ablest pupil at "gym". And I am reminded too of that gravestone which used to fascinate me as I wandered through St Mary's churchyard close to my junior school. The epitaph read, "As you are now so once was I. As I am now so you will be". Thankfully, God remembers the strengths and the labours of our youthful and active years, though to the younger generation they are unimaginable.

146

## An Eventful Year

The most important event of all in my life – that I would be "a good girl", as my mother expressed it, and become a Christadelphian – was a foregone conclusion, both by my parents and myself. No other course of action ever entered my head. Mum and Dad were not at all happy when one of my twelve-year-old Sunday School friends was baptised for, as explained earlier, "it didn't do" to be baptised too young in view of the responsibility of accepting "the Truth". Encouraging me to delay the vital step of immersion must have been a difficult stand for my parents to take, since death before baptism would have dispelled their hope of my resurrection to immortality.

"Putting my name in" was delayed until I was eighteen, longer than it need have been – caused by awe of the ceremony and of the "entrance examination". I must only have just "passed" that ordeal for in my anxiety, and despite the encouraging kindness of the examiners, the name of Abraham's son quite escaped me. Had I been examined, not by two Brethren, but by a large group or by the whole ecclesia, as some candidates were, then I would have forgotten many more well-known facts, and would, I fear, have long remained one of the aliens to which Grandad was so wont to refer.

My eventual decision was not prompted by any blinding light on the road to Damascus but by the courage of lifelong friend, Beryl Miller, who, eighteen months younger, decided to take the important step. We were baptised on the same day. The meeting welcomed both of their new members joyfully, and no doubt felt rewarded for all the loving care and teaching which they had bestowed on the two children nurtured among them.

On the following day I returned to the Post Office Savings Bank "born again", though, in fact, in my way of life and in my heart (and like Beryl) I had never been anything other than a staunch Christadelphian. But now born "of water" I joined enthusiastically in the activities of the ecclesia, the many meetings, the special efforts, distributing *Glad Tidings,* giving talks at the Mutual Improvement classes which were attended by both Brethren and Sisters, and enjoying the happy fellowship of the Finsbury Park members.

**Ruth Ward c. 1940**

# XXV
# ALL CHANGE

## We Move House

My parents, having saved enough to obtain a mortgage, managed to promote the family to home ownership and a modern house. So, with our Heacham benefactor, George Alcock, advising on the paperwork, we moved from Palace Road leaving behind all its palatial inconveniences, the black leading and the step whitening, my little laburnum tree and Grannie's Jenny Creeper, taking with us memories of joy and sorrow.

Grandad was still with us and we moved into our new "electric" residence at 58 Ashridge Gardens, Palmers Green – a road lined with cherry trees. And Mum and Dad who had never owed a farthing, who had always paid for everything on the dot, now owed most of the hundreds it cost. But they also "owned" their little "semi" with even a "dining room". Now with every modern convenience, there were no fragile gas mantles to be lit. The magic switch lit every corner, and as a candle was no longer needed to light me to bed, there were no spooky recesses where might lurk 'a chopper to chop off my head'. As Aunty Daisy would have said, "Fancy that!". And as we switched on and off, fancy that we did. But to leave a light on which we did not immediately require was unthinkable. We still had to save our pennies (which usefully helped to save earth's resources).

## A New Friend

In so enormous an establishment as the Post Office Savings Bank, inevitably there were interspersed among the staff a number of those who professed Christianity. "Birds of a feather", they say, "flock together", and though as a Christadelphian I would not have counted those individuals as genuine Christians, nor as having feathers with the lustre of

149

my own, yet they were receptive to discussing the Christian faith, and, of course, I saw it as my duty to preach "the Truth".

May Bennett was a colleague and one of the gentlest of girls whose presence seemed to breathe the love of Christ. I was well acquainted with our community's contention that people in general merely accepted every belief presented to them in their churches without questioning. So when May explained to me that she thought of the Godhead as being like a jug of water poured out into three glasses, I realised that her erroneous notion was simply the explanation she had been taught. I was very sorry (once again) that so worthy an individual was not on the road to salvation, and regretted her lack of understanding which could have such "awful consequences" (as Robert Roberts has described it). But, as always, there was the comfort of my let-out clause. Christ was at the door and May, I was sure, would be among the first to accept him and to have her false doctrines corrected.

The office provided one particular situation which merits more than passing comment. A new girl called Margery appeared in the Stock Branch. She was about my own age. Perhaps from our first acquaintance we both knew that we were different from our colleagues, and it was not surprising, therefore, that during the morning break we joined company. This Margery now provided me with a similar problem to the problem I met in my school days – only more so.

She was another of those individuals, like myself, who believed that her parents knew "the Truth" and that only *their* "Truth" was true. But this time both her parents and mine were dedicated Christadelphians, each with a different hierarchy of Brethren which guided its own group of ecclesias. Each set of leaders disapproved of the other, though Margery and I were little acquainted with the differences which separated them and which prevented our participating together in the memorial service. We had, it seemed, both been born in the same belfry, she on one side and I on the other. She had, of course, accepted second-hand "what she had been taught at home, and in the ecclesia" (to use Robert Roberts' words again), just as I had, and, I suspect, like myself "without ever giving it a thought whether it was right or wrong". It was all rather disconcerting but we decided it was better to be friends than to try sorting out the difficulties which apparently none of our betters could do. Shortly afterward, at evening class, I met Helen Light (née McGregor) and her sister (another) Margery. They, too, had been brought up on the "other side". Friends we could be but share the bread and wine together we could not.

That this situation existed in the Christadelphian community was not, of course, news to me, and doubtless not to my new friends. I could recall my mother's indignation after one of her Temperance Hall Christadelphian cousins visited and announced in the course of conversation, "Purity before peace". In retrospect I realise that the points of view of both Mum and her cousin were understandable. Their mothers (from the family of thirteen children) had left Marlow to go into service in London. Both had encountered Christadelphians and both married into "the Truth". When in 1885 the community was rent in two, the sisters had been divided, each with her respective husband, one on one "side" and one on the other. Whether either Grannie or my Great-aunt understood the complexities of the division is highly improbable. But rivalry had been born, and the children had been born into it as well as "into Christ", and therefore had followed their parents, as young people then were more inclined to do than they are today.

There would have been many members like them, members who were not able to appreciate the significance of the arguments put forward by the leading Brethren on either side, nor those by the other groups which developed. Most "average" members adopted the policy of whichever "leading light" they preferred, either because of the accident of their birth or because they admired one character more than the other. Even today, after so long a cooling-off period, it is not easy to ascertain from extant material the full cause of the damaging division.

## "Changed life is now our Portion"

The Post Office was never a popular Civil Service Department. More interesting work and more opportunities for promotion were available in other parts of the Service. So when I was transferred to the Board of Education in Whitehall it was seen as a distinct advantage. But with my usual conservative approach and dislike of new circumstances, at first I was far from happy. The ministerial corridors of power and the whole environment seemed alien and awesome. Whereas today three-year-olds are at the ready to pick up a phone and, if necessary, call the emergency services, I, unaccustomed to making or receiving calls, found the black apparatus sitting on the desk, with its potential to pose enquiries on secondary education which might or might not be out be of my depth, positively threatening. Oh for the confidence and competence of my grandchildren!

However, during the closing years of the 1930s, the more momentous fear than answering a telephone was threatening the world at large, as already explained. Big Ben was booming reassuringly, yet round the corner at No 10 there was increasing anxiety. Passing the Cenotaph each morning and evening had become part of my daily routine, though the solemn reminder it held of the catastrophe which had convulsed Europe twenty years earlier and to which it bore witness meant little so far as I, personally, was concerned.

**Kensington Science Museum**

# XXVI
# THE END OF ERAS

Despite the age of fourteen being the time when most children left school to begin their working lives, official adulthood was not then attained until the age of twenty-one. By 1939 my "childhood" was fast drawing to a close, and drawing to a close, too, was the twenty-year era of "peace in our time". The Board of Education was moved to Kingsway, possibly because, with the threat of war, education was no longer a priority, and Whitehall was required for the expansion of the departments more relevant to the critical international situation. The new accommodation was situated opposite the imposing Air Ministry headquarters. That was not the most desirable of locations in the circumstances, though our office basement had been converted into a reinforced air raid shelter to which shortly we would flee from time to time.

Soon staff were not only being conscripted into the Forces but some were being shunted into the Defence Ministries, and before long the Board was to be evacuated to Wales. I was appalled at the thought of leaving London, for I wished to stay at home in the familiar places with the familiar faces where no harm could come to me, encased, as I thought, in my shell-proofed holiness. I therefore had the temerity to explain to my senior officer that I did not wish to join my colleagues, unable as I would be to join in their activities. Probably that didn't surprise him, for oddity that I was, I had already announced that I didn't belong to England but to Christ. But it does surprise *me* with hindsight, that during so extreme a national emergency, the likes and dislikes of such small fry as myself were given any consideration. But they were, and obligingly I was moved to the Science Museum in Kensington which was under the Board's jurisdiction.

The dimly lit Museum was closed to the public and though there were some cheery souls among the staff, it carried a feeling of "Ichabod", desolation and departed glory. The government order of longer working hours was soon introduced (even if we were not busy) and a ban on heating (except from the staff's chain smoking) soon added to the discomfort of the environment. The occasional exercise of running up and down stairs to improve circulation helped out. And in the basement the workshops, instead of creating artefacts for museum exhibits, were manufacturing parts for aircraft.

Now, instead of making daily excursions past the Cenotaph, I was making my way round the archaic aeroplane sitting brooding, as it were, in the gloomy gallery. Human beings are fantastically clever with their ability to advance in technology, but if that contraption had remained undeveloped, then much of the horror which was descending on the cities of Europe, the destruction of their architectural beauty and the annihilation of their inhabitants (including Christadelphians) could never have occurred. The scientific revolution which brought benefit to the people of the world had brought also the power to destroy themselves.

## "The end is where we start from"

Whatever disasters occur on the national front, for those relatively unaffected and wrapped up in themselves as I was, personal affairs at all times loom the larger. A year or so previously, in the spring of 1938, and of no consequence to the world at large, a young Scot whose "childhood" was also drawing to a close, had reluctantly left the land of his birth and arrived apprehensively at King's Cross. He was met by Brother Stan Gibbins waving *Glad Tidings*. The newcomer was in readiness to take up a post at the Home Office in Whitehall.

George McHaffie

154

It was not long before search-lights would be flashing through London's black-out in search of enemy aircraft. And the next six years would witness the deaths of millions across the globe. But for me, in my little world, the new arrival at King's Cross station was to become a star, a star which would change my life and brighten my existence for over forty years. And when at last, and all too soon, it faded from sight, and when, in retrospect, I appreciate more than ever before how much its shining meant to me, I was left with many "thoughts that do often lie too deep for tears" – and much else besides.

But that leads on to another story.

[Continued in the second part of Ruth's autobiography *Reformation and Renewal*.]

# Appendices

Some additional pieces by Ruth are added here, plus the published obituary and an extended family tree.

Appendix 1

# The Star of the Grass
(Ruth's first printed article,
in *The [Christadelphian] Young Folks' Magazine*, 1936)

## THE STAR OF THE GRASS

We are inclined to despise such flowers as dandelions and daisies, and to pass them by as "just weeds." If you have ever stopped and looked closely at the golden flowers of the dandelion you will have found how truly wonderful they are. Each of what most of us call a petal is a flower, and the dandelion is a number of the small florets. So you see that the dandelion is even more wonderful than the larger flowers, and perhaps you have never noticed.

There are a number of people in the world who are very like this flower. They do not show you at first all the gifts they have and how good they are, because they do not boast. Rather than display themselves, they prefer to be trodden down, and to remain unnoticed. If, however, they are called upon to do something we find them ready. Perhaps we have not noticed them before, and yet all the time they have been working and doing those things which are pleasing to the Almighty God. We should try to be like this, humble and yet doing all those little deeds of good.

The next time you find a dandelion, do not despise it as a weed, but look closely and you will find that the little star of the grass is trying to show you the love of God and that it is glorifying its Father in Heaven who made it and all that is upon the face of the Earth. Then after that perhaps you will be able to find some people just like that—"Stars of the grass," who are also showing others the love of the Almighty and who are patiently and in works with faith, finding an entrance into the Kingdom of God which will one day cover the face of the whole earth.

Ruth M. Ward

# A Reputation for Gentleness
(Written in the early 1960s)

On the first occasion when I was to visit my son's new school he thought it desirable to give me some instructions. "When you come charging up to the school..." he said. I felt obliged to protest that I had no intention of "charging up," but hoped to approach with the inoffensive demeanour expected of a harmless parent. Later it occurred to me how very descriptive was his schoolboy phraseology of the manner which we sometimes adopt towards others.

It is not surprising if the approach of one schoolboy to another is clumsy and if differences between the two of them provoke animosity. Nor is it surprising if men and women whose god is Self become antagonistic toward one another under the slightest provocation. What *is* surprising is that so often since the founding of the Christian Church, many of those who have claimed to obey the God of Love have shown just as much bitterness and antagonism toward those whose theological opinions have differed from their own as have any worldly counterparts. They have considered it part of righteous Christian warfare that they should "charge up" to their spiritual opponents, committing even physical violence against them.

We ourselves are not moved to commit violent atrocities and we would all lament them, but bitterness because of opposite opinions still rears its ugly self, and though it may be exhibited by us only in a refined way, it is yet sadly deplorable. Perhaps the most surprising fact of all is that even when we know how wrong such behaviour is, even when we outwardly restrain ourselves, yet there will be few hearts amongst enthusiastic stalwarts, which, if honestly searched, will never reveal a seed of bitterness quietly germinating in time of opposition. That we should "let all bitterness, and wrath, and anger, and clamour, and evil speaking, be put away" and that we should be "kind to one another, tender-hearted, forgiving one another," are precepts easier stated than observed. Sometimes we find "angry young men" (and women!), disheartened by the unloving spirit which they feel others show, calling so loudly and so vehemently for more love amongst us, that their very cry becomes bitter. What strangely confused creatures we are! How much, in our weakness, we need the forgiveness and saving grace of our Lord!

Yet we have reason to rejoice. Now, perhaps more than ever before, there is a stronger feeling amongst us that we must be less dogmatic, less self-assured, and more humble in our lifelong search for truth. We are more ready to consider fairly, opinions which are new to us, realising that we cannot expound Scripture with apostolic authority, but that, in company with others, who are equally sincere, we can but present the truth as we believe it to be. There is a greater desire amongst us to have "a reputation for gentleness" (Phil. 4:5 – J. B. Phillips), a quality to which the apostle Paul exhorted the believers of his day.

Looking back some sixty years ago we find our grandfather of strong conviction. He did not believe in hiding his light under a bushel and he was willing, even eager, to stand against opposition. He was forthright in his arguments and was apt to be vehement in his pronouncements against those who opposed his beliefs. Some of us may even look back with a shudder at the way grandfather attempted to present the gospel to "the alien," and remember that if his rheumatism prevented him from attending the business meeting, there to add his forceful contribution, then his family saw his indisposition as an ill wind that blew somebody some good!

Possibly it is only to our own younger days that we need to look back to find hardness. Perhaps we used to believe that the truth could be tied up in a neat parcel, and because of youthful idealism, which lacked loving understanding, we were bigoted and intolerant of the views of others, and therefore heedless of our Lord's pattern of forbearance. But maybe we have grown in grace so that today there are more of us saying, "Let us do away with hardness and have more love." We try to affirm our convictions in a kindly way and, by our behaving more pleasantly in ecclesial relationships, it has been made possible for us to have reunions instead of divisions, and differences of opinion without disfellowship.

Yet we have lost something! We have lost a liveliness which our grandfather had. However much we may dislike the more aggressive attitude of some nineteenth century believers, we cannot but admire them for their vitality and for their determination to stand up for what they believed to be right. They were people who *cared* and they cared greatly.

We live in an age of "couldn't care less" and we are influenced by the atmosphere of our day. It is not always our Christ-like love which enables us to allow others their opinions: quite often it is our apathy. If we have lost our vehemence, is it not possible that we have also lost our "go"? And are we not in danger of exchanging vital enthusiasm for sleepy insipidity?

The task before us is difficult. To have the spirit of crusade together with the spirit of peaceableness has been the duty of every Christian in every age, but, always, only a few have risen to it. Could we not, now, make a determined effort so that more of us can become ardent soldiers for Christ and yet acquire that "reputation for gentleness"? Could we not remember, more often than we do, that as the "captain of our salvation" won His victories by love, so also must we?

Our brother John Thomas left us a stimulating heritage. He it was who wrote deprecating those "who would discourage or throw hindrances in the way of free, unbiased and independent examination and avowal of Bible truth" (*Elpis Israel*). He made every effort himself to examine the accuracy of his faith, and his example is an encouragement to each one of us.

If, with our Father's help, this magazine can create an atmosphere in which we can carry on that "independent examination," being unafraid of finding truth, but much afraid of losing love, then it will do well. If, in its lines and between its lines, there can shine the spirit of honesty, forthrightness and enthusiasm combined with gentleness, meekness and humility, then it will achieve something which is very great indeed.

(*Endeavour*, No. 1, Summer 1961, pp. 4-5, written without any expectation that within a year she, with her husband George, would be called upon to take over the editorship.)

## Appendix 3

# A Family Concern
(Written in the early 1980s)

"No hawkers, no circulars" read the notice on the gate. Deciding that I was neither a hawker nor a circular I went up the garden path. But, no, the lady opening the door would not like to make a contribution to Oxfam. Back down the path, resisting the temptation to add a sticker on the gate, "Oxfam is a family concern. Share in it.", I tried next Door. There I was greeted by a charming young man, wrapped only in a bath towel. Undaunted by his damp and chilly condition he retreated briefly, returning to add his bit of weight to my plastic "tin".

Going from door to door asking for donations during Christian Aid and Oxfam weeks is not the most entertaining nor pleasurable way of spending an afternoon. The uncertainty as to one's reception, when, after many an odd noise, the doors are cautiously opened, is disconcerting. But the misery of deprivation in the Third World stands as a challenge. And as I shiver in Edinburgh's keen wind, the coldness brings to mind the misery of those in other countries who, less well equipped, inadequately clothed and fed, have to face far harsher elements.

Usually householders give a kindly reception, and donations are gladly made. Some who refuse are themselves having genuine difficulty in coping with their meagre resources. Some others are blunt and rebuffing with their refusals. How to reply to these I am never sure. No doubt they have their reasons for not wishing to help, and maybe I should ask what they are. Perhaps I should try to explain more about my mission. To say "Thank you" is inappropriate, and merely to say "Oh" seems inadequate. At least I am now convinced that I should not feel personally rejected but that I should feel rejected on behalf of those who cannot ask help for themselves.

Apart from the purpose of the collection, the work is not altogether dull nor without interest. At the quieter doors, where there is no large dog eager to meet or eat me, no small child delighted to receive a sticker (blissfully unaware of his good fortune to be born in the affluent part of the world), then, while the household purse is found, I study the entrance and garden.

There is the variety of home decoration, the exotic colour scheme and the quality of workmanship. "Do-it-yourself" is often evident. I note that, in spite of my husband's criticism of my handling a paint brush, other amateur efforts are not necessarily better than mine and some are decidedly worse. That lovely run down the door is a rival to any of mine!

I observe that the occupiers of well furbished homes and well groomed gardens are not necessarily the most generous subscribers, and they sometimes refuse altogether. A frayed carpet and shabby furniture can be regarded as good signs, for the owner may well contribute one of those much coveted pound notes, or even a fiver. A lesson, perhaps, in having the right priorities.

With a gardener's eye I regard the mass of weeds in the rose bed. But my feelings are mixed and not altogether disapproving. I remember the uninvited ground cover surrounding my own roses – and am glad that the inability to control the natural unruliness is not mine alone.

In one garden a favourite but rather rare perennial thrived luxuriously. I paused to admire the vivid beauty of its flowering. The lady of the house assured me that many neighbours had been given roots but none had succeeded in establishing it. If only I could try! If only I dared to ask for just a tiny piece! After all, a fellow collector had been given a rose which she had admired. But, come, come, Madam. You are collecting for Oxfam, not for the herbaceous border.

How different one's own locality looks from an unaccustomed angle! Sheltering from the rain in the new neighbouring flats, I glanced admiringly from a landing window at the flower bed beyond. Whose should it be but my own! – with distance lending enchantment to the view, and not a weed (in sight). Another lesson here? Do we become so familiar and even discontented with our own possessions that we fail to realise that we have it so good? While we groan about inflation and the cost of living, finding it difficult to maintain our houses, cars or what have you, perhaps we fail to realise how fortunate we are to have even so much as a roof over our heads?

One lady making a donation seemed to apologise for not giving more. "I go to Oxfam", she said. Puzzled at first by her meaning, I afterwards presumed that she meant she frequented an Oxfam shop – perhaps to assist, perhaps to buy, perhaps to give. With Christmas coming near, that festive bonanza when we exchange with our friends cards, and gifts that we do not need and probably do not like, perhaps more of us could "go to Oxfam": before Christmas to make our purchases, after Christmas to deposit our unwanted gifts.

Finally, the afternoon's collecting is over, and it is home for tea. It will be scrambled egg – but who in the family minds? There is plenty and enough to satisfy our needs. For us, the "haves", there is not only jam for tomorrow, but also jam for today. But for the "have-nots" there is no jam at all.

## Appendix 4

It took the family a long time to succeed in persuading Ruth to use a computer. Once she had mastered it, she worked on it almost every day. The phrase "tim'rous beastie" is from the poem written in 1785 by Robert Burns: "To a mouse, on turning her up in her nest with the plough".[41])

# Grandma and the Computer

## The "wee, sleekit, cow'rin', tim'rous beastie" – and Grandma

"I'm glad you're not in my class", said my daughter. Come to that, so am I. But in this new age and on the inadvertent press of a button, my 'preference' is ignored, my size 'reduced', 'invisibility' comes into view and there stand I – the new recruit for Primary 1.

So what have we here? Every infant a chooser, free-ranging round the "green" classroom while I, having the edge over them of some three score years and ten, yearn for an

---

[41] Wee, sleekit, cow'rin', tim'rous beastie,
O what a panic's in thy breastie!
Thou need na start awa sae hasty,
      Wi' bickering brattle!
I wad be laith to rin an' chase thee
      Wi' murdr'ng pattle!

I'm truly sorry man's dominion
Has broken Nature's social union,
An' justifies that ill opinion
      Which makes thee startle
At me, thy poor earth-born companion,
      An' fellow mortal!

allocated, fixed spot, my eyes searching in vain for the cheery card on the wall with its reassuring "a" for apple.

Plucking up courage I venture from the shelter of the book corner, timidly tap Miss S and ask for its whereabouts. She points to an object which I, in my ignorance, had thought to be the school TV. "I'm helping James at the moment", says she, "He's having a problem with his reading" (no wonder!). However, given a minute or two, she would help me bring up "a" on "the monitor". I do my best to comprehend, recalling that once, long ago, I, myself, was the class monitor (and a highly commendable one at that). But on a piercing shriek arising from the direction of the said object Miss S abandons James and investigates, only to find that the shrieker has "lost" half his story. However, all is not lost (nor even half) for her magic touch recovers it, and relative peace is restored.

She starts talking about a mouse. Hope for me yet? But no, it's not "singing", and anyway, I suppose Animal Rights wouldn't approve of heads being cut off with a carving knife. To my astonishment the whole class has halted in its tracks, and for once unbroken silence reigns.

Messy paintbrushes and sophisticated art-in-the-making have been abandoned. Everyone is assembled and sitting comfortably on the carpet square, cuddling up to Miss S, sticky thumb in mouth if required. She proceeds to deliver an uncommonly severe lecture relating to the atrocious crime committed by some monster who switched off the mouse. They all nod knowingly (including the unidentified culprit), and all appreciate the disaster likely to befall the community through such dastardly behaviour. A non-operative mouse, I discover, means no down-loading and no running off of the newsletter so eagerly anticipated by pupils and parents alike. And by what other conceivable means of communication was it to be conveyed to home hearths that Colin's Daddy has bought a new car and that Clare's Mummy has bumped into it? Hopefully the powers-that-be will soon provide a mouse-trap for any who wish to indicate to others in the workplace that they have switched off. That would make the whole process more user-friendly.

So intent was concentration on the ill-treatment of the 'wee, sleekit beastie', that on rising from the carpet and resuming individual pursuits, one red-faced young man is now standing in a puddle. A system error, perhaps? Everything is so unreliable these days and not in keeping with the standards to which I am accustomed. By contrast, however, to the annoyance of Miss S over the mouse, this latest occurrence is apparently of little consequence, for as she kindly explains in a loud voice to wide-eyed spectators, "We all have accidents".

We proceed to "environmental studies". Once more attention is riveted on Miss S in an attempt to view at close quarters her thrilling exhibits dug up from the long-distant past. An archaic writing book is produced, and amazement is expressed that she, reared in the age of the dinosaur, had difficulty in getting her "b's" and "d's" respectively facing in the right direction. But despite the evidence of the photograph and two, genuine, well-preserved plaits complete with red ribbons, the whole concept proves inconceivable. Gratitude is felt all round when one chubby-face inquires whether, when she was at school, she was a boy or a girl. After all, the class caterpillar had turned into a moth, so how was a fellow to know all the exciting possibilities of this wondrous world?

Weeks have now passed. Miss S, who perceives that I am not relating well to my peers, takes me along to the cosy room of the Lady in High Command. We discuss my aims and objectives, my strengths and weaknesses (especially my weaknesses) and it becomes apparent that, assisted by an enor-mouse file, forward planning has been done on my behalf in keeping with the five to fourteen guidelines and, of course, in my best interest. It seems that to save me from total defeat in the mouse-race I am to be gently ejected. I am to quit and go to "special" where all my latent talents will come into view, and my feeble style emboldened.

Privatisation could be the answer but only if I am sure that such a programme is in keeping with my choice. And, surprise, surprise, Miss S volunteers to be my "key worker". She is convinced that on a one-to-one basis in the home environment I am educable and just tolerable. "It would make your writing so much easier", she promises.

Knowing the scorn of many an old friend in relation to newfangled devices – ("They even use them in the church!" they say), I tread cautiously lest I am being enticed by cheese into a trap. But at last, chivvied along, I (by now usefully enlarged to A3), gingerly set out on the yellow brick road to "find" the Wizard of Oz.

As is altogether suitable during my declining years, other members of the family have now turned into free home-helps and supportive care-workers. Even the labelled teenage giants, who only yesterday were of the lap-top variety, prove invaluable when my masterpiece of prose is in danger of extinction owing to a recalcitrant computer.

Annoying though it is to find that my spelling (so laboriously mastered) can be checked at the touch of a button, and some of my innocent vocabulary declared "illegal", there are definite advantages. Even if a trifle inelegant, apparently it is still within the legal limit if I opt to "skip" and I am able therefore to preserve that particular skill acquired over the years. In addition, I am usefully called to attention should I inadvertently overrroll my "r's". Moreover, without my becoming a drookit rat on wet mornings, my loads of rubbish are emptied with alacrity, not just on council collection days but whenever I choose (even on high days and holidays).

And by now, despite the ups and downs and having to work long and hard at it, my "cow'rin, tim'rous" self has persuaded the all-powerful mouse to establish a stable relationship with his "poor earthborn companion". And with the two of us being wholly compatible with each other (but not, of course, with all and sundry), no panic strikes our 'breasties'. Fortified on every side with piles of back-ups we have no fear that our 'best laid schemes' might 'gang a-gley'. And we can even put Miss S right on a thing or two!

Appendix 5

# Obituary

## Ruth McHaffie (1920-2004)

Ruth, along with her husband George, edited *Endeavour* from 1962 to 1967. In addition to articles and editorials, Ruth also contributed the prayer on the inside back cover and sometimes some of the art work. This was not her first writing. She produced a hand-written handbound book at the age of 15 on *Christ, The Messiah,* and her first printed article was contributed to *The [Christadelphian] Young Folks' Magazine* at the age of 16.

In earlier years she wrote regularly in *The Christadelphian* and in the *Christadelphian Youth Magazine.* After George died in 1985 she began working on some of his material, but soon became involved in research of her own. She was a meticulous student, accessing a large range of sources in the National Library of Scotland, New College Library (Edinburgh University) and in the British Library in London. She built up a wide knowledge of post-reformation religious history and thought, and made a detailed analysis of Christadelphian writings. This resulted in her first major book *Finding Founders and Facing Facts* (2001), and in *Timewatching and Israel,* a two volume work which was still at the printers when she died but is now available. She completed her final two books, *Cradled in Christadelphia* and *Born to Reform,*[42] two days before her death. They are a spiritual autobiography, charting her upbringing, with comments and observations on the community, the changes in thought and doctrine over the years, and why she believed reassessment is necessary. These are still on her computer, but it is hoped to have them printed

---

[42] [Subsequently retitled *Reformation and Renewal.*]

later this year. An ALS leaflet, produced shortly after her death, also includes some of her writing.

Ruth was not a bookish person, despite her literary output. She brought up four children, and delighted in her seven grandchildren and five great-grandchildren. She worked at the Citizens' Advice Bureau, became a social worker, and almost every day from 1969 until 1997 was involved in the day-to-day running of the old people's home set up by Edinburgh Ecclesia. For 35 years the Ecclesia met in a hall attached to her house, which meant she was part-time caretaker there too. She regularly and reliably set out the bread and wine. It was she who found new premises for the Ecclesia when they expressed a desire to own their own hall, and she contributed in a major way in helping to decorate and furnish it.

She was well known as a lively and spiritual speaker at the New Year Gathering. One sister remembers how she began an address to a sisters' class in England: "If a job is worth doing, it is worth doing well. That applies to religion as well as in other areas of life." With George she produced one of the first write-ups in the brotherhood to advocate a wider involvement for sisters: *The Work of Sisters in Gospel Fields*. Four years ago she proposed the motion, arising from proposals at ecclesial discussions, that sisters should read at Sundays meetings. This was approved and is now established practice.

After she was told she had terminal cancer, she maintained a cheerful outlook and her committed concern for others. She said: "I'm 83 and I've got to die sometime. I've had a good life, a good family, and I have my faith. It's all right." She pushed on right to the end, working with greater urgency over the last year when she realised her health was deteriorating.

Ruth loved nature, especially flowers. She did some gardening almost every day. She produced oil paintings, mostly of scenes with flowers and trees. But her major involvement was always in caring for others.

She was very much a person who put her Christian thinking into positive action: she collected in the annual street collection for Christian Aid until prevented by ill-health. She played the organ for hymn singing at a local old people's home. In hospital she maintained this concern, helping to look after the other patients! She kept in touch with a wide circle of friends including some of those she had helped as a social worker, and others who contacted her through her writings. She was easily approachable: you could discuss anything with her, and receive a helpful, sympathetic response. Her hospitality has been enjoyed and remembered over the years. She wrote frequently to others, or phoned "for a chat" and to see how people were; latterly she began to use email for longer distance communication. She will be missed by many. One wrote to her a month before her death: "You are such a good friend, and a very caring person. This world would be a much nicer place if there were more Ruth McHaffies in it."

However, in herself she was unassuming and modest. She didn't want a funeral service – "Just a few words at the grave side", she said. Persuaded otherwise by her family, she chose the hymns, but suggested "Any good things they say about me should be taken with a pinch of salt."

After her funeral a letter was received from the local council: her request that they install a seating-rail in the bus stop across the road had been acceded to. It is there now.

Her work lives on in her kind deeds, in her writings, and in the memory of those who have benefited from knowing her. She sleeps now in Christ, her Messiah, her Saviour. We give thanks and praise to God.

(Reprinted from *The Endeavour Magazine*, No. 111, June 2004)

Photo on Saturday 2 March 2013 in Garden at 180 Granton Road, Edinburgh, on occasion of Party for Heather's 60th Birthday which was on Wednesday 27 February 2013. Those named in italics are Ruth's direct descendents.

**Back Row** (left to right): Matthew Crich, *Rosalyn Crich (née McHaffie)*, Ross Lindsay, *Peter McHaffie*, Sophie McHaffie (née Etherington), *Ben McHaffie*, *Jonathan McHaffie*, *Neil McHaffie*, *Attie McHaffie Lindsay*, *Charlotte McHaffie*. **Inset** (at top left): *Stuart McHaffie Lindsay* (born 10 August 2013)

**Middle Row**: *Ian McHaffie*, *Lauren McHaffie*, *Alexander Crich*, *David McHaffie*, *Amy Haddow*, *Abigail McHaffie*, *Kathryn Haddow*, *Lucy Haddow (née McHaffie)*, Tim Haddow, *Steven McHaffie*.

**Front Row**: *Stephanie Crich*, Camille McHaffie (née Marshall), Deborah McHaffie (née Bottomley) holding *Leo McHaffie*, Hazel McHaffie (née Hayles) holding *Rory McHaffie*, *Heather McHaffie*, *Matthew Haddow*, Averil McHaffie (née Howe), *Isabella McHaffie*, Fiona McHaffie (née Young) holding *Oscar McHaffie*, Janice McHaffie (née Adams).

---

Family tree:

RUTH WARD (1920–2004) — M 1943 — GEORGE McHAFFIE (1920–1985)

Children: IAN, DAVID, PETER, HEATHER

**IAN** — M 1971 — AVERIL HOWE
- LUCY — M 1996 — TIM HADDOW
  - Kathryn (2000), Matthew (2005), Amy (2002)
- CHARLOTTE — M 2008 — ROSS LINDSAY
  - Attie (2010), Stuart (2013)

**DAVID** — M 1968 — HAZEL HAYLES
- JONATHAN — M 1997 — CAMILLE MARSHALL
  - Abigail (2000), Lauren (2002)
- ROSALYN — M 1999 — MATTHEW CRICH
  - Alexander (2003), Stephanie (2005)

**PETER** — M 1971 — JANICE ADAMS
- STEVEN — M 2002 — DEBORAH BOTTOMLEY
  - Rory (2007), Leo (2010)
- NEIL — M 2008 — FIONA YOUNG
  - Isabella (2009), Oscar (2013)
- BEN — M 2012 — SOPHIE ETHERINGTON

**HEATHER**

177

## Appendix 7

# A Prayer for Understanding

Help us, Father, to understand the true worth of eternal
values:
Help us to know that material things are but as snowflakes
which melt in the sun.

Help us to understand being in the world, bearing its burdens
and sharing its sorrows;
Yet not being of the world, craving its lusts and seeking its
follies.

Help us to understand one another, our differences of
thought, character and circumstance:
Help us to know how to help in times of sadness, strain and
difficulty.

Help us to understand the needs of the young who are in our
care:
Help us to know how best to guide them into the paths of
truth.

Help us to understand the weakness of human nature:
Help us to know Thy greatness and the strength of Thy
power.

Help us to understand the inspiration of Thy Word, and the
indwelling of Thy Spirit.
Help us to understand being temples fit for Thee.

In the name of our Lord, Who understands all,
Amen.

(Ruth McHaffie, *The Endeavour Magazine*, No. 15, Spring 1965)

179